D1483355

Custom Harley

Custom Harley

Barnes & Noble Books
New York

This edition published by Barnes & Noble, Inc.,
by arrangement with Book Sales, Inc.

2004 Barnes & Noble Books

This edition produced for sales in the U.S.A., its territories, and dependencies only.

M 10 9 8 7 6 5 4 3 2 1

ISBN 0-7607-6233-3

This book was designed and produced by
Quintet Publishing Limited
6 Blundell Street
London N7 9BH

Designed and Edited by Q2A Solutions

Publisher: Ian Castello-Cortes
Associate Publisher: Laura Price
Creative Director: Richard Dewing

Art Director: Roland Codd
Project Editors: Jenny Doubt, Catherine Osborne

Manufactured in Singapore by Provision Pte Ltd
Printed in Singapore by Star Standard Industries Pte Ltd
The material used in this publication previously appeared in *Custom Harley* by T. Remus, *Harleys, Popes, and Indian Chiefs* by T. Paulson and F. Winkowski, and *The Harley-Davidson Legend* by M. Norris.

Contents

Down Memory Lane

No question about it, there is a mystique attached to the Harley-Davidson. A love of Harley-Davidsons begins the moment you sit astride one and fire it up for the first time. A prod of the starter button and the engine instantly comes to life, the steady beat of the pistons keeps time with your pounding heart, and the throaty exhaust note sucks the breath out of your body. A tentative twist of the throttle and the machine responds with an apocalyptic roar. This is an awesome experience never forgotten.

It is now that you realize this is no ordinary motorcycle that you are riding. This is a living beast, and you'll be in that state of euphoria for days afterward, as you begin to plan just when and how you're going to get your hands on one of your own.

This book reveals how and why the Harley-Davidson remains the last and greatest American motorcycle ever made. And as for the Harley-Davidson mystique, well, the only way to understand fully what it is, is to own one.

Down Memory Lane

When Bill Harley and Arthur Davidson began experimenting with motorized bicycles in 1901, they had no idea about the legend they were kickstarting.

The Silent Gray Fellow

What Harley and the Davidson brothers built in a backyard shed in 1903 bears little resemblance to the Harleys seen today. It is often said that the carburetor on their earliest bike was fabricated from a tomato soup can.

The first bike was seen to be underpowered, which was remedied by beefing up the single-cylinder, inlet-over exhaust engine to a stalwart 30 ci (494 cc) in 1906. Then, in 1907, leading link forks were added, giving the model improved handling that was so successful the same design was retained until the development of the Hydra-Glide Harley in 1949. Another crucial alteration was the replacement of the crude leather belt drive with a more maintenance-free chain drive.

The bike that resulted from these simple changes pointed the way to the familiar configuration and look that would be reinforced in the following decades. At the same time, the simple frame reveals its origins – the metamorphosis from bicycle with engine to full-fledged motorcycle had only begun.

The name Silent Gray Fellow was bestowed by designers William Harley and Arthur Davidson on all the bikes their company produced up until World War I. "Silent" referred to the efficient, sound squelching mufflers with which the early Harleys were equipped. "Gray" was for the flat gray paint job that distinguished these bikes. "Fellow" was intended to invoke the dependability of the machine.

The First V-Twin

In 1909 Harley-Davidson introduced its first V-twin, but it was quickly withdrawn, suffering from problems with the intake valves. In addition, because there was no tensioning device on the belt drive, the leather drive belt was unable to handle the extra power. (It is surprising that a tensioner device was not fitted straightaway, for it was already available on the singles being made at the time.) The V-twin was re-introduced in 1911, with new

Right **The first Harley-Davidson only came in black with gold striping. In 1906, a Renault Gray finish was also available.**

HARLEY-
DAVIDSON

Above **A 1915 V-twin. From 1903 to 1920 Harley-Davidson made about 175,000 of their early singles and V-twins. They were also the only manufacturer to guarantee the horsepower on their motorcycles.**

mechanical inlet valves and a belt tensioning device that helped to transfer the power to the rear wheel. This also meant that the belt could be slackened so that the engine would idle and not die when the motorcycle came to a halt. Although this device worked well, a larger version of the V-twin (61 ci/1,000 cc, previously 49.48 ci/811 cc) was available from 1912 with a chain drive.

This model, the 8-E, also featured Harley-Davidson's first clutch, which was installed in the rear hub. Thus the rider could pull away from a dead stop without having to pedal at all.

The Sport Twin

In 1919, at a time when most American motorcycle companies were concentrating on producing large V-twins, Harley-Davidson tried to fill a gap in the middle-weight market by introducing the Sport Twin.

The model was a 35.6 ci (584 cc), with cylinders horizontally opposed fore and aft, much like the Douglas, the British motorcycle produced in models of this type.

This bike came as a great surprise to the rest of the industry, not just because it was a departure from the V-twin, but also because it was rather dull to ride. With a top speed that might just make 45 mph (73 kph), the only advantages this machine had were the almost vibration-free ride that it gave, and the accessibility it allowed to the engine for maintenance.

It was hoped that the Sport Twin would attract many new riders, but unfortunately for Harley-Davidson, Indian introduced its 37 ci (600 cc) Scout at the same time, and not only was it much more powerful, it was also a V-twin, which even in those early days was already regarded as the traditional American motorcycle. Although the Sport Twin did not appeal to the American public, it was successful in Europe.

The First 74s — The FD and JD (F Heads)

In 1921, to herald the new decade of optimism, the first 74 ci (1,200 cc) V-twin was introduced. With its larger engine and greater power, it was more suitable for sidecar work than the 61,

Below **A 61 ci (1000 cc), 61J model. The "olive drab" paint was the only color available for most of the 1920s, although by 1928 Harley-Davidson had ceased painting the crankcases.**

as well as being rival to the infamous Indian 74.

Like the 61F and J models that had been launched two years previously, and that had evolved from the first 1909 V-twin, these 74 ci (1,200 cc) V-twins came in two versions – with magneto ignition (model 21FD) or generator (21JD). For the 1928 season a sportier version of the single cam J model was introduced, namely the R (61 ci/1,000 cc) and the JDL (74 ci/1,200 cc).

This year also saw the arrival of the much-lamented "two cammers," the JH (61 ci/1,000 cc) and the JDH (74 ci/1,200 cc). These "two cammers" are still regarded by many as the best of the old V-twins that the company ever produced. However, although they were good for their time, they were usually not as perfect as some enthusiasts would have you believe, mostly because they were inclined to overheat and break down when ridden at sustained high cruising speeds. Sadly, they were all discontinued in 1930 when the new model V was introduced. However, the J model did manage to continue in Class C competition until 1936.

The year 1928 is also notable as the year when Harley-Davidson fitted front brakes to a bike for the first time, although they were initially only on the big twins.

The 1,200cc Model V

The 74 ci (1,200 cc) was virtually all new, sharing only a few parts with its F head predecessor. Despite weighing a massive 550 lb (250 kg), over 100 lb (45 kg) more than the F head, it was capable of a similar top speed, 80–85 mph (129–137 kph).

Although many "two cam" enthusiasts still maintain that their mounts were faster than the new model V, and that they were continually asking the factory to re-

introduce them, few disagree that the old F heads were temperamental and unreliable. They may well have become better than the new V – had they remained in production for more than two years so that there was an opportunity for their faults to have been ironed out. But the

Below **The side valve model V was produced between 1930 and 1937. From 1933 onward, a variety of Art Deco tank designs and new colors were introduced. Below is a beautifully restored 1934 VL and sidecar.**

few surviving motorcycle magazines of the times were mindful of their small circulations and were not about to upset their main advertiser, so they toed the company line by promoting the new model V as a significant improvement over the "two cammers."

The V series eventually appeared in approximately 13 different guises. It is not possible to be more precise, for Harley-Davidson frequently introduced new models that had only slight cosmetic variations and that did not even appear in some catalogs. Nevertheless, the principal models were the standard V and the VL with slightly higher compression, and two versions equipped with a magneto, the VM and VLM. With the introduction of the dry-sump lubrication system in 1937, the V became the U (U, UIL, and so on), and just before that, a 80 ci (1,340 cc) model was released (the UH and ULH).

As had been the case with the 45 ci (750 cc) D model, the V series was brought out prematurely after insufficient testing, and no sooner were the machines leaving the showroom, than they were breaking down. The factory was inundated with complaints, and further deliveries of new machines were suspended. Within weeks a new engine design was in production with larger flywheels, new crankcases, valve springs, clutch plates, and a modified frame among other improvements. Although dealers received a package to modify the motorcycles they had sold, they were not recompensed for the time it had taken them to rebuild their customers' machines.

Coming so soon after the problems with the initial 45 ci (750 cc) machines, this naturally caused great resentment among the dealers, as well as some loss of faith among customers who had purchased one of the earlier troublesome motorcycles.

The 500 cc Model C

This 30.5 ci (500 cc) side valve single was available with an optional hand clutch, and was offered between 1929 and 1934. Like the 21 ci (350 cc) Peashooter, it was never a strong seller in the United States, where a 45 ci (750 cc) V-twin was considered the minimum engine size.

It was first placed in the 21 ci (350 cc) Peashooter frame, but later shared the frame of the 45 ci (750 cc) model and, unfortunately, also the clutch and gearbox that had caused so many problems. Tests were made on an overhead valve version of this single, but the plans for this were shelved.

Harley-Davidson had an on-off relationship with both the model C and the smaller 21 ci (350 cc) single. One year they were not sold on the

home market, but reappeared two years later. The model CB appeared for only a short time, in 1933–34, and was really the 30.5 ci (500 cc) single in the 21 ci (350 cc) frame. At the same time, the 21 ci (350 cc) model B side valve made a brief return.

Around 1930, 74 ci (1,200 cc) machines managed to account for approximately 53% of sales, with 45 ci (750 cc) machines and singles representing 30% and 17% of sales respectively. By the end of the 1920s over 40% of production was exported, but soon after 1930, import taxes were raised in Australia and New Zealand, which were major markets for the singles. Soon after, the effects of the depression spread throughout the world and exports quickly dropped to 10% of total production.

Above **A car mechanic stands by his Servi-Car. His tools were carried in the large box at the back of the bike.**

The Servi-Car

The three-wheeled Servi-Car first emerged in 1932, and remained in production right up to 1974.

It was fitted with the 3-speed 45 ci (750 cc) D model engine, which powered a sprocket on the rear axle by a single chain. It was aimed at the light utility market, and it sold in large numbers to garages, which could send out mechanics on one with all their tools in the large box behind the rider, to work on a car and, if necessary, attach a tow bar and bring the car back. It was also employed by many police forces for traffic work. You can still see examples hard at work today in some Indian cities, where they have been converted into taxis and can now carry up to eight people, if not in comfort, then certainly in great style.

The Knucklehead

After much research and testing so as not to repeat the side valve mistake, the first overhead valve V-twin came on to the market in 1936.

This 61E model (61 ci/1,000 cc) was the direct ancestor of today's successful Evolution engine.

Below **The direct ancestor of today's Evolution engine, the 61E was considered an amazing machine for its time.**

The Knucklehead, as it came to be known (the shape of the rocker boxes on the right of the engine resemble the knuckles on the back of a hand), had many new features, some of which are still found on today's Harley-Davidsons, more than 50 years later.

For the first time Harley-Davidson installed a dry sump (oil circulating between the engine and oil tank) rather than a total loss oil system, with the horseshoe-shaped oil tank located underneath the seat and a 4-speed constant mesh gearbox, and the whole engine contained within a double-loop frame. The gas tank was welded instead of soldered and was in two halves, with the speedometer set into it (like the modern Softails). Further important developments to the 61E were a full valve enclosure in 1938 and a 74 ci (1,200 cc) version – the 61F in 1941 – which could achieve 100 mph (160 kph).

The WLA 46 ci (750 cc)

Harley-Davidson had already produced a military version of its 45 ci (750 cc) DLD for testing by the United States Army before war broke out in Europe in September 1939, and shortly afterward the company received an order to supply 5,000 military motorcycles for the British Army, because British manufacturing capacity had been destroyed by German bombing.

Painted in gloss olive green, which was quickly replaced by matte olive green, this model was redesignated the WLA and was equipped with ammunition boxes, skid plate, rifle holster, luggage rack, and blackout covers on the lights. Mechanically, these bikes proved to be virtually indestructible. With their low compression, low speed – 50 mph (80 kph) was the maximum – and substantial torque, they proved, during service with the Allies' armies, to be highly reliable and capable of enduring sustained abuse.

The Panhead

The Knucklehead was replaced by the Panhead in 1948, but it retained the model designations E and F for its 61 ci (1,000 cc) and 74 ci (1,200 cc) versions.

The introduction of the Panhead started a trend that continues to this day – the modern Evolution engine was developed by fitting a new top end onto the existing Shovelhead engine; the Shovelhead had a new top end fitted to a Panhead engine; while the Panhead engine featured a new top end fitted to the bottom half from the Knucklehead. The name Evolution, therefore, derives from the engine's evolution from the Knucklehead. Some small and important changes were made over the years to enable these transitions to be made. Full details of these changes are included in excellent books by either Allan Girdler or Jerry Hatfield.

The most striking visual difference between the Knucklehead and the Panhead was the aluminum heads, which resemble baking pans. These enabled the engine to run cooler and helped to keep the engine oil-tight. Despite many improvements, some of the problems with the all-iron Knucklehead were never resolved, and they still suffered from overheating and oil leakage around the rocker boxes. Inside the Panhead many refinements had been made. Hydraulic lifters removed tappet noise, a larger pump improved the flow of oil, and there were no external oil lines.

Below **The military version of the WL model (the letter "A" after the WL designated the army version). The Canadian Army version, the WLC, can be easily distinguished from the American Army version, the WLA.**

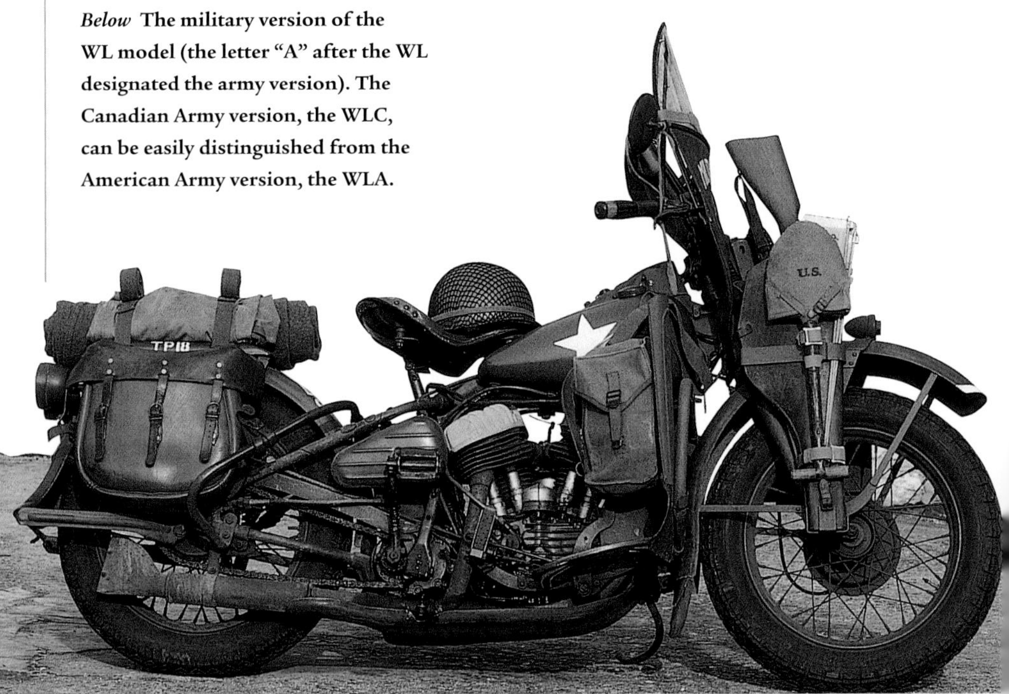

Above **A 1957 FL that was purchased from the Vietnamese government in 1989, exported, and restored.**

Further important developments on the Panhead were made in 1949 when telescopic front forks were used on the Hydra Glide, in 1952 when the optional foot gearshift was added to the FLF, and in 1953 when the distinctive trumpet-shaped air horn was first used. In 1956 high lift cams were introduced; in 1958 rear suspension was used on the Duo-Glide, and in 1965 an electric starter was developed for the Electra Glide.

The standard 61 ci (1,000 cc) E and 74 ci (1,200 cc) F had been dropped by 1952, and the rest of the 61 ci (1,000 cc) E models, EL, ELF, and ES, had disappeared by 1953.

The XA 45 ci (750 cc)

During this period, the American Army was testing the XA, of which it had asked Harley-Davidson to build 1,000. The XA was a copy of a BMW 45 ci (750 cc) side valve twin, with horizontally opposed cylinders and shaft drive.

It was designed for use in the desert, because a shaft drive motorcycle would be more suitable for sandy terrain than a chain-driven machine. However, the four-wheel drive jeep entered production at this time and was deemed more suitable for this purpose, so the XA project was terminated.

Lightweights

Harley-Davidson had received many requests from their dealers for a 21 or 30.5 ci (350 cc or 500 cc) bike to compete with the British motorcycles that were being imported in increasing numbers. The company responded by saying that it did not have the capital to develop a new model. Instead, it introduced a 3-speed 7.6 ci (125 cc), which was a copy of the German DKW. Soon afterward, the British manufacturers BSA produced its own copy, which was called the Bantam.

This little two-stroke was aimed at school boys and for light utility work and, with the aid of a finance package, could be purchased for $5.50 a week.

It was the first of several 7.6–10.7 ci (24–175cc) lightweights, which were produced from 1947 onward. Many of these had cute names such as Topper, Bobcat, Hummer, Ranger, Pacer, and Rapido – the 3-4 ci (50-65 cc) machines were known as Sport and Shortster. Some of these lightweight models were made at the Aermacchi plant in Italy after Harley-Davidson had taken it over in 1960.

The K Model

Production of the WL was finally terminated in 1951 after 22 years of service. Its replacement, the model K, appeared in 1952, looking very much like its modern European competitors, with a swing arm, rear suspension, telescopic front forks, left-hand clutch, and right-foot gear

Left **The 7.6 ci (125 cc) Hummer that appeared in the late 1950s. This was a slightly updated version of the first lightweight that Harley-Davidson had made in 1947.**

change. It was, however, powered by a side valve engine of unit construction that was based on the 45 ci (750 cc) V-twin, which had first appeared in the 1920s. With a top speed of 80 mph (129 kph), it was far slower than its smaller overhead valve competitors. A sportier version was quickly developed by blending the K with the racing KR to produce the KK.

To improve performance the motor was enlarged from 45 ci (750 cc) to 55 ci (883 cc) two years later, and this KH model could achieve a more respectable 95 mph (153 kph). The KHK derivative was the "hotter" street bike.

The K was regarded as a disappointment when it was first released. It arrived just when buyers wanted an American motorcycle that could compete with the smaller 30.5 ci (500 cc) Triumphs and BSAs, and although later versions sold better, the bike was generally regarded as a stopgap until the factory could produce something

Left **A 1954 55 ci (883 cc) KH model. While the KH was significantly better than its 45 ci (750 cc) model K predecessor, the sportier KHK was the only version that offered serious competition to the British bikes on the street. The original bikes in good condition are extremely rare.**

that could really blow everything else away.

It says a lot for the talents of Harley-Davidson tuners Tom Sifton and, later, Dick O'Brien that the racing version of the K, the KRTT, won at Daytona on its first outing there in 1953, finishing far ahead of the second bike home. It won its last race there in 1969, too, and to rub it in, Cal Rayborn even lapped the rest of the field.

Although the racing KR stayed competitive for 18 years until it was replaced by the XR-750 in 1970, the road-going model K lasted only four years.

The Sportster

In a way that was reminiscent of the development of its big twins, in 1957, Harley-Davidson designed a new 55 ci (883 cc) overhead valve top end and fitted it to the K engine. This new XL engine was slipped back into the K frame, named the Sportster, and, with a few other changes, sent out to repel the invasion of British motorcycles.

It was a great success right from the start, achieving twice as many sales as the K in the previous year. True to form, Harley-Davidson introduced a higher compression version – 9:1 compared with the XL's 7.5:1 – and fitted larger valves the following season, when they called it the XLH.

Even this boost in power was not enough for many, and the factory was inundated with demands from dealers for an even faster version. For once the public got what it wanted, and the XLCH arrived late in 1958. This sporting version was sold with high-level pipes, a magneto ignition, semi-knobbly tires, and the small peanut tank that is, today, standard on Sportsters. The standard XL power output was 40 bhp, but the XLCH produced 55 bhp and was capable of exceeding 120 mph (193 kph) and .25 mile (400 m) times of 14 sec. This model, unsurprisingly, was soon outselling the standard XL, and it was many years before anything else appeared that could match its performance.

The XLCH was tamed over the years, and despite an increase in size to 61 ci (1,000 cc) in 1972, the top speed was slowly reduced, and buyers switched their attention to the now almost as fast, but more civilized XLH. Production of the XLCH finally ended in 1979.

Other variations were the XLX, a very basic 61 ci (1,000 cc) Sportster, the XLT touring version; and the XLS Roadster, which was styled after the FX Lowrider. There were also two "hot" Sportsters. The XR-1000, which was styled like the successful racing XR-750 with twin carburetors on the right and the exhausts running high along the left side, was basically a standard XL 61 ci (1,000 cc) engine with the XR-750 heads engineered by Jerry Branch. At 6,995USD (3,992GBP) it did not find many buyers, and those who were interested in performance invariably purchased the 3,995USD (2,240GBP)XLX, and fitted the hotter twin carburetors, cams, alloy heads, and exhausts themselves – and still had plenty of change left over.

Like the XR-1000, the XLCR that was introduced in 1977 lasted for only two years. This all-black Cafe Racer could reach 120 mph (193 kph), but did not sell to the sporting rider and was not considered a "real" Harley-Davidson by those who thought they knew best.

Below **The XLCH was initially intended for off-road use, and came with these high-level exhaust pipes. Later versions had the short dual pipes that became traditional on Sportsters. The bike was blessed with a strong gearbox and a clutch that seemed indestructible, even when drag racing.**

The XL Sportster is still with us, however, even more than 35 years after it was first introduced.

Aermacchi

In 1960 Harley-Davidson purchased a half share in the struggling Italian Aeronautica Macchi Company, which produced motorcycles. Soon after the deal was made, the first of the Aermacchis arrived in the United States. It was renamed the Harley-Davidson Sprint. This four-stroke 15.24 ci (250 cc) single could top 70 mph (113 kph), and by 1967 it was Harley-Davidson's biggest seller, while the 21 ci (350 cc) version that arrived in 1969 and could exceed 90 mph (145 kph), sold almost as well. In 1972 these four-strokes were replaced by two-strokes from the Aermacchi factory, but by 1977 the Japanese had taken over the market for two-strokes, and Aermacchi was eventually sold back to the Italians.

The racing versions of the model C Sprint – the

Above The four-stroke Aermacchi Sprints came in both 15.24 ci (250 cc) and 21 ci (350 cc) engine sizes. In 1968 a tuned 15.24 ci (250 cc) version of this single exceeded 177 mph (285 kph) at Bonneville.

Left Only 3,000 XLCRs were ever made. The new frame had a triangular rear subsection and suspension that was derived from the racing XR-750.

Above **1976 FLH.**

CR, CRS, and CRTT – were frequent winners in the short-track races in the United States, while the two-stroke versions, the RR 250 and 350, were ridden to four world championships on the Grand Prix I circuit by Walter Villa.

The Shovelhead

The Panhead gave way to the Shovelhead in 1966. This was topped with alloy rocker boxes, which were very similar to those that had first appeared on the iron head Sportster in 1957. Its nickname came about as the covers were said to look very similar to the back of a shovel.

The later Panheads had external oil lines, which were continued on the Shovelhead. For the 1970 model the generator was exchanged for an alternator inside the primary case, with a new cone-shaped timing cover, giving rise to the names Generator Shovels and Alternator Shovels (Cone Motors). In 1978 the 80 ci (1,340 cc) version was introduced.

The Shovelhead continued to have the same designations on the basic models as that of the Panheads –

the FL and FLH – but one of the most striking differences between the new Shovelhead FLH and its 1952 FL Panhead predecessor was in the weight. The FLH weighed a massive 783 lb (355 kg) when fueled up. There were many variations on the now standard 74 ci (1,200 cc) FL. The H was boosted another 16 hp to 60 bhp and was loaded with the touring extras; the F featured the foot shift; the B was fitted with an electric starter; the P was the police model; and the T had a 5-speed gearbox and a new rubber-mounted frame.

The B designation was dropped in 1970, when the electric starter became standard equipment, and the F disappeared in 1973, when the hand shift was no longer offered.

The FX

The FXS Low Rider: The wheelbase was lengthened, the seat was lowered by over 2 in. (5 cm) and the foot rests

Below **The 1971 FX Super Glide with the fiberglass seat. A similar seat unit was also offered as an option for the Sportster that year, but this attracted few buyers. This giant leap forward in design for Harley-Davidson was ready to go into production in 1967. However, only when AMF had taken over was the go-ahead given.**

Above **Close-up of the modern 80 ci (1,340 cc) Evolution engine.**

moved further forward. It was also equipped with siamesed two-in-one exhaust pipes, special paintwork, mag wheels, and flat drag handlebars.

The FXEF Fat Bob: This was fitted with the fatter 5 gallon (23 liter) fuel tanks that had appeared on the first FX but were replaced on later models by a slimmer 3.5 gallon (16 liter) tank. It also had a shorter, bobbed rear fender.

The FXWG Wide Glide: Basically a Fat Bob with slightly longer and wider front forks and a 21 in. (53 cm) front wheel, 2 in. (5 cm) larger than the standard FX. What really set this bike apart were the flames painted on the tanks that imitated the custom trend at the time.

The FXB Sturgis: This was a Low Rider, but with a black chromed engine and black paint work. It was powered by belt drive, not chains.

Some of these models had a 74 ci (1,200 cc) engine, but they were all eventually offered with a larger, 80 ci (1,340 cc) engine.

The Xl Sportster

Still around after all these years and available in four models with 55 and 74 ci (883 and 1,200 cc) engines, the XL Sportster now comes with the 5-speed gearbox and belt drive on the 74 ci (1,200 cc) and 55 ci (883 cc) deluxe that are fitted on all of the 80 ci (1,340 cc) models.

The V2 Evolution (EVO)

This was the first option in the new range, and it came out in

Below **A 1989 XL-1200. The original exhausts have been replaced with accessories that do away with the balance pipe that obscures the beautiful V-shape of the engine.**

1983. The Evo engine was so called because it had evolved out of the Pan- and Shovel- and Knuckleheads and had a new top end fitted to the bottom of the old Shovelhead engine.

It first appeared on the FX, and spread across the rest of the range over the next three years. Today Harley-Davidson makes only two different types of engine, both of them Evos – the Sportster, which internally comes in two sizes, and the second type of engine, the 80 ci (1,340 cc), which is fitted to the rest of the range. They appear in the 18 bikes that Harley-Davidson sell.

The FL Tour and Electrica Glides

The five Glides have the engine isolation mounted, and they differ from each other only in the quantity of fiberglass and gadgets that are added on – the top of the line models even come with a cigarette lighter.

The FXDB Dyna Glide Sturgis

The limited edition Sturgis first appeared in 1980. It was basically an all-black Super Glide with a belt drive installed instead of a chain. So successful was this that belts gradually replaced chains across the range. The Sturgis was brought back in 1990 and installed in a new chassis with isolation engine mounting. For 10 years Harley-Davidson bikes had a balance pipe running between the two exhaust header pipes, and this cut across the distinctive V-shape of the engine. With this model the company found a way to tuck it out of sight.

The FXS Softail

The four Softails take their styling from an earlier age with their bobbed or traditional rear fenders, chrome wrap-around oil tank, and a rigid-looking frame. The FLSTC Heritage Classic has a transparent windshield, studded saddle bags, and front fender, which imitates the look of "dressers" from the 1950s. The FXSTS Springer takes this look back even farther with the sprung front forks that appeared on a Harley-Davidson in 1948.

Left and Right **1990 FXSTS Softail Springer. The rigid-looking frame and modern Evolution engine create a perfect blend of the old and the new.**

SHOEI
SHOEI
Harley
WARRS
Davidson
1
DUNLOP
Kendall

Harley in Racing

During the formative years of racing, when manufacturers were competing fiercely to win races with factory-sponsored teams, Harley-Davidson chose to remain apart. Although individual enthusiasts would enter, and often win, on a Harley-Davidson, they received no assistance from the factory. And then, much to the riders' annoyance, the company would boast in its advertisements that its machines were so good that they could win races without any support from the company. In 1903 motorcycle clubs founded the Federation of American Motorcyclists (FAM). It took several years for the FAM to be accepted. But by 1908, it was able to announce its first major event, a two-day endurance run around New York and Long Island. Needless to say that Harley-Davidson bikes emerged the clear winner, enhancing the company's claim that its bikes were the most enduring, reliable, and stylish mode of transport around.

Harley in Racing

Noticing the increase in sales that followed early competition successes in 1908, the company decided to enter the sport formally.

To design racing motorcycles and set up a racing team, Harley-Davidson enticed William Ottoway away from Thor in 1913. Working with William Harley, Ottoway began by modifying the 61 ci (1,000 cc) pocket valve roadster, which was produced for the public. This tuned roadster was christened the Model II-K.

In 1915, for the first time, Harley-Davidson team riders appeared on the winner's rostrum when team captain Otto Walker and Red Parkhurst took the first two places in the 300 mile (483 km) road race through the streets of Venice, California, on 28 March, averaging 63 mph (101 kph) around the 3 mile (4.8 km) course.

July 1915 also saw one of the team's most celebrated victories at the Dodge City track. Riding the 61 ci (1,000 cc) pocket valve V-twins, Otto Walker crossed the finishing line first, with five of his team-mates in second, fourth, fifth, sixth, and seventh places.

This Harley-Davidson team came to be known as the Wrecking Crew. From 1916 the team increasingly dominated racing, until, in 1921 it won every single national championship – six of them at record speeds.

Unfortunately, just as the Wrecking Crew hit its peak, sales of new bikes slumped, and at the end of 1921 the team was disbanded.

Meanwhile, there was widespread agreement that the larger motorcycles were too powerful for the circuits on

Left **Joe Walter aboard a 61 ci (1000 cc) V-twin at the Speedway Park board track in 1915. Many of the races on these tracks were run over 300 miles (482.79 km).**

Above **This restored 1929 JDH parked outside a church uses "Police Blue" paint – one of six color options in paint available that year.**

which they raced, and that something had to be done to reduce the number of accidents. In response to this, in 1924 and 1926 the Motorcycle and Allied Trades Association changed the rules governing Class A races. Following this, the Harley-Davidson Peashooter ridden by Joe Petrali dominated both short track and hill climbing. In 1931 Petrali signed up with Harley-Davidson, and went on to become the national champion in 1931, 1932, 1933, 1935, and 1936.

Class C racing was introduced in 1934 in a bid to revive public interest and to encourage amateur riders back into the sport. Engine size was limited to 45 ci (750 cc) for side valves and 30.50 ci (500 cc) for overhead valve machines, with Novice, Amateur, and Expert categories for riders.

Class C racing rapidly became the most popular form of competition. Noticing the resurgence of interest, both Harley-Davidson and Indian began to develop new 45 ci (750 cc) side valve V-twins. Indian delivered the Sport Scout and Harley-Davidson first the WL, and in 1941, the WR.

With the WR, Harley-Davidson first used its particular style of designating the racing versions of its production bikes. The W was the stock bike that the customer purchased; the WIZ was the dirt track model; and the WRTT was the version equipped for road racing. Shortly after the WIZ was introduced World War II intervened, and all competition was suspended until 1946.

The K model made its racing debut in 1952, and for the first time featured a hand clutch, a foot shift on the right, swing arm, and shock absorbers.
Like its predecessor, the W model, it was also a 45 ci (750 cc) side valve, and, because the heads of the engine were squared off blocks of aluminum, it became known as the Flathead.
The dirt track version was known as the KR, while the KRTT was for road and TT racing.

The KR arrived on the scene in 1952. Toward the end of the year the first KR's were winning races, and early in 1953 Paul Goldsmith, riding a KRTT, won the Daytona race for Harley-Davidson for the first time in 13 years.

Sadly, this was also the year in which Billy Huber died from heat prostration while leading the 200 mile (322 km) race in Dodge City. Billy was unwittingly, responsible for the small peanut gas tank on today's stock Sportsters. This came about when he substituted the 4.5 gallon (20 liter)

Below **WR model built from scratch with virtually all-new parts. The owner has no intention of ever starting it up.**

Above **1968 KRTT ridden by Dan Haaby at Daytona that year. This was the first time that the Harley-Davidson colors of black and orange were used on the racing team bikes.**

tank on his KR for the smaller, 2.5 gallon (11 liter) tank taken from a 7.6 ci (125 cc) Harley-Davidson two-stroke. It was adopted by the rest of the team, then by customizers, and it was eventually offered on the Sportster.

In 1954, Joe Leonard won the championship by coming first no fewer than eight times in 18 races on a KR tuned by Tom Sifton. The following year the Leonard/Sifton KR engine was sold to the 19 year-old rookie, Brad Andres, who not only won the Daytona 200 with it but also the championship for 1955. For several years this winning streak continued unbroken. This golden era came to a close in 1962, however, when Resweber was forced to retire from the sport after receiving serious injuries in a pile up during practice at the mile track at Lincoln, Illinois, an accident that also claimed the life of Jack Goulsen.

For many years Harley-Davidson dominated domestic racing. But by the late 1960s the tide was turning. Japanese and British bikes started to win races. This forced Harley-Davidson to build a successor to the outdated K model. The need for a new racing bike could not have come at a worse time, for the company was in dire financial trouble. The solution was to take the 55 ci (883 cc) XLR and, by de-stroking it, reduce its capacity to 45 ci (750 cc). This was then slotted into the KRTT low boy frame and christened the XR-750. Equipped with an iron head (cast iron cylinders and barrels) and single carb, this was hardly more powerful than its predecessor, the KR.

Stylistically, the new XR-750 was a great success; mechanically, however, it was beset with problems. For the first time the British and the Japanese manufacturers could pit their 39 ci (650 cc) and 45 ci (750 cc) bikes against the Harley-Davidsons, and for the last time qualifying was determined by which bikes were the fastest. None of the Harley-Davidsons could qualify for any of the first 10 places on the grid.

At the end of the season, for the first time since the competition's inception, a Harley-Davidson did not occupy first or second place in the final championship placings.

The 1971 season was equally disappointing. In 1972 the rejuvenated version of the XR750 arrived. After modifying the weaknesses inside the engine, the bore was enlarged and the stroke shortened to produce an over-square engine. Both carburetors were located on the right of the engine, and both exhausts ran high along the left side. To crown the whole package, the iron barrels and heads were replaced by alloy versions with wider and more numerous cooling fins, hence the name Alloy Head. This new version was immediately successful, and by the close of the season Harley-Davidson was back on the winner's rostrum.

During the early 1970s Japanese-made two-strokes, swamped road racing, and also threatened to take over the dirt track when Yamaha unleashed its 4-cylinder TZ 45 ci (750 cc) two-stroke. After Kenny Roberts wrestled the bike to its only dirt victory at the Indy Mile in 1975, the AMA brought in a new rule that only 2-cylinder engines were eligible for dirt track races.

***Left* The XR 1000 was styled on the XR-750. This 1984 model has received many modifications, including the red paintwork.**

Above **The popularity of the 55 ci (883 cc) Sportster racing is spreading throughout the world, and England, too, now has its own series. Pictured here is Grant Leonard who, when not racing, is a motorcycle journalist.**

Throughout the rest of the 1970s Japanese bikes dominated road racing, while the XR-750 still had the edge on dirt tracks.

During the 1980s, both Yamaha and Honda had introduced their own V-twins to contest the dirt races, but they enjoyed little initial success. However, Honda started to get things right, and as a result, between 1984 and 1987, managed to come out on top. The rest of the decade, was all Harley-Davidson's, and as the 1990 season ended, the XR-750 entered its 21st year of competition.

The American Twin Sports Series began in 1989, and in its second year, such was the interest from riders and spectators, it could already boast a season of 34 races. It was exclusively for 55 ci (883 cc) Sportsters, which could be slightly modified, and run very much in the spirit of the original Class C rules. The great attraction of this type of racing is that all the machines start off equal, the winner is the person who is the best rider, as well as being the person with the most innovative tuner. Sportster racing provides some of the closest, most exciting, not to mention the best sounding, racing around. This is in the true spirit of Class C racing.

Custom Harleys

Looking back on the early days of customized Harleys, most people recall only the psychedelic images of "choppers" from 1969 and 1970 – Panheads with extremely long springer forks and metal-flake green paint jobs. What many of us forget is the fact that the choppers evolved from earlier motorcycles, and that those earlier bikes set the stage for the bikes we remember so well. An absolute starting point might be an arbitrary thing, but the Second World War makes as good a beginning as any as thousands of returning GI's came home with money in their pockets, and bought motorcycles. Many bought the same bike or brand they saw during their time in Europe. Thus there were Harley-Davidsons on the streets during the 1950s and 1960s, but there were also plenty of Triumphs and BSAs.

Evolution of Custom Harleys

Many of the early Triumphs were customized with a smaller gas tank, a trim seat, and a Bates headlight.

The idea was to simplify the bikes, eliminate anything unnecessary, and replace the necessary things like handlebars with parts that had more class. The Harley owners were doing very similar things to their bikes. Even before the war, riders were installing the longest of the factory front fork assemblies, though no one was changing the fork angle at that time. Front fenders were removed and the rear fender was trimmed or bobbed, and in the slang of the day these simple pre-choppers were known as "bobbers."

The aftermarket for parts started after the war, when, for the first time, you could buy parts for your bike somewhere other than the local dealer. One of those new stores, the Flanders store in Pasadena, California, offered an extensive line of accessories, including higher, narrower bars and the parts needed to adapt them to then-current Harleys.

Motorcycle slang

The new handlebars went higher and higher until riders were nearly standing up to reach the handle grips. They looked like apes hanging from a tree. Names and slang terms like "ape-hangers" evolved on the street, and became part of the two-wheeled culture.

At the other end of the bike a sissy bar gave the passenger a backrest. These sissy bars, combined with either ape-hangers or pull-back bars, helped to define the custom bikes being built in the late 1960s and early 1970s. Open any early chopper magazine from the period and you'll find bikes that established a look and style that remains popular to this day.

Harley-Davidson riders started with a "74," essentially a full-size Knuckle- or Panhead, and stripped off anything that wasn't essential. Hardtail frames were the order of the day. At the front a long, extended fork supported a 21 in. (53 cm) front wheel.

Riders sat low on the bike, with legs outstretched to reach the highway pegs. A contoured seat provided support for the back. Harleys were considered the best of this breed, though plenty of Triumphs and Hondas were modified with hardtail kits, high bars, and extended forks.

Chopper magazines

By the late 1960s and early 1970s motorcyclists of the day had a number of magazines to choose from, each one filled with parts to buy and articles explaining how to install them correctly. The list of available parts was quite extensive and included complete hardtail frames, extended tubes for glide forks, springer fork assemblies, and a hundred smaller items.

Even though anyone could construct a bike with new parts, some people developed a reputation for

Above **Looking like something that should be parked in an art gallery, this Arlen Ness custom uses unique sheet metal components fabricated by his old friend Bob Monroe.**

building complete bikes with hand-fabricated parts. Men like Arlen Ness, Dave Perewitz, and Donnie Smith became professional custom builders.

Magazines like *Street Chopper*, *Chopper*, *Big Bike*, *Modern Cycle*, *Supercycle*, and *Easyriders* began to cover the best of the bikes and carried ads from a hundred new companies.

A water-stained copy of *Street Chopper* from 1970 features a chopper from San Bernardino, California, equipped with a "thirty over" fork, 21 in. front rim with Avon tire, blue metal flake paint job, tall sissy bar, and a bobbed fender.

The movie that inspired the look

If one event immortalized the look of a long stretched-out motorcycle, it was the movie *Easy Rider*. Peter Fonda's bike set the pattern that is still followed today: Rake the frame

and extend the forks. Design the seat to put the rider down low, add forward controls and a sissy bar. Finish with plenty of chrome and a bright paint job.

Easy Rider captured the look and spirit that riders and builders had been working toward for 20 years. Various motorcycle fads have come and gone since then, but the popularity of that particular look refuses to go away. Open a copy of any current custom motorcycle magazine – retro choppers are back in fashion, right down to the springer forks and Panhead engines.

The bikes changed through the years. Gas tanks got smaller ,and forks became longer. Neck angles were altered to 40 and more degrees. The small Mustang tanks were often molded into the frame. At first the really cool bike was a Knuckle- or Panhead – then Sportsters, and finally Panheads and Shovelheads, took center stage as the coolest place to start when constructing a chopper.

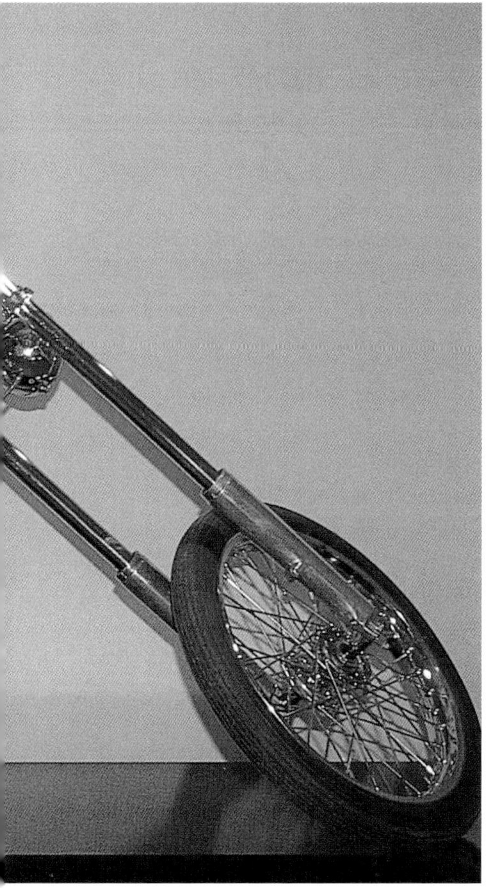

American exports

American riders weren't the only ones craving and building choppers. Europeans and the Swedish bikers in particular, developed a fondness for

Left **This Easy Rider replica was built by Paukis Harley-Davidson in South Germany. More than any other single machine, this bike created the chopper craze, which in turn helped spawn the current passion for custom Harley-Davidsons.** ***Horst Rösler.***

long Harley-Davidsons. While the laws in countries like Germany wouldn't allow any radical customizing, the Swedes had more freedom to alter fork angles and install fabricated parts. In fact, when choppers fell from popularity in America in the 1980s, the Swedish builders continued to make choppers.

Death of the choppers

By the early 1980s people stopped building the wild custom machines. As the customers stopped building and buying, the chopper shops closed or evolved into normal service facilities.

In retrospect the blame can be laid, in part, on the soft American economy at the time. Perhaps because of this, motorcycle sales took a nose dive at the start of the new decade. The other reason people stopped building bikes was simply because they didn't have to any more. By 1980 you could buy a factory-built custom from Harley-Davidson – a bike with extended forks, more rake, a 21 in. (53 cm) front tire, padded sissy bar, and a red-on-black flamed paint job.

The flamed Harley-Davidson Wide Glide from 1980 was the first in a long line of custom bikes built at the Harley-Davidson factory. Milwaukee had, until that point in time, ignored the trends, but starting with the Wide Glide, Harley-Davidson began genetic transfer on a corporate scale.

From Wide Glides the factory quickly moved to the new Softail bikes. By using a triangulated swing arm the new Softail had the look of a Hardtail without the harsh ride. The first true factory cruiser was created by pairing the new pseudo-hardtail frame with more of the California-Classic styling cues seen earlier.

The creation of the Softail and all the models based on that frame was the best marketing move ever made by Harley-Davidson. The Softail chassis serves as the foundation for at least four families of very successful bikes. Before that time Harley had the engine, what could be described as the ultimate American motorcycle power plant. With the addition of the Softail line, Harley-Davidson had the sound and the look that defined an American motorcycle.

The mid and late 1980s were not a good time for custom bikes or the aftermarket industry. Customizing your bike meant making few changes such as adding chrome accessories or repainting the sheet metal.

Right **Two of Arlen's earliest surviving motorcycles, a Shovelhead and a Sportster. Note the struts, wild paint, and handlebars on the Sportster, and the overall simplicity of both machines.**

CAL
BK4899

Around 1990 the tide turned and riders began once again to make an individual statement with their motorcycles. Though the young riders have aged, each one still needs a Harley, and each of these machines needs to be different than all the rest. People wait for two or three years to get a new Harley. Once they own the bike the stock sheet metal comes off, replaced by new parts and fresh wild paint schemes.

Milwaukee is working hard to meet the demand for bikes. At the same time, they're introducing new custom parts and accessories to compete with the huge aftermarket. Farther down the line the small custom shops are looking for larger facilities and more fabricators.

Each of the best-known customizers has forged a relationship with a large aftermarket corporation. Rick Doss works with Custom Chrome, while Don Hotop designs for Drag Specialties. In addition to their work with the best-known builders, each of these companies buys designs from freelance fabricators and designers.

This corporate recognition seems an affirmation of the important role these individuals play in a very healthy industry. Without them there might not be four or five major companies selling everything from taildragger fenders to billet aluminum running boards. They set the styles, create something for all the riders to shoot for, and provide proof that it can be done.

European bikes and bikers

Europeans have always ridden motorcycles. More recently they've discovered Harleys and custom Harley-Davidsons in particular. When the Barbican Gallery in London put together an exhibit called "The Art of the Harley" in early 1998, they brought in customized Harleys from both America and various European countries. British, German, French, and Swedish builders contributed to the exhibit with a variety of designs: everything from brutally fast German bikes to the long extended shapes of the Swedish choppers.

Each country has its own style, dictated partly by taste and partly by regulation. German laws are strict, and the bikes tend to reflect that with alterations that are more conservative than those found on other European bikes. The Swedes build choppers, and the French create elaborate flowing designs painted in bright colors.

Setting the record straight

New riders from either continent, astride their first Sportster or Softail,

Left **This flathead uses foot clutch and a hand shift on the left side of the gas tank.**

tend to think this whole phenomenon is relatively new. However, the best-known designers and busiest shops all have roots that date back to the 1960s and earlier. In fact, the whole wave of success being enjoyed by both Harley-Davidson and the aftermarket can be traced back to those exciting days of yesteryear. Unable to leave their machines alone, those first fabricators set the stage for a phenomenon none of them could have foreseen at the time. Rick Doss and Arlen Ness started designing bikes back in the 1970s, and have witnessed the rising popularity of customized Harleys. Bikers have always pushed the boundaries of Harley design—whether it's raking the frame or pushing the front wheel out ahead of the bike.

Customized Harley-Davidsons have become both a craze and an industry. The passion to create a personal motorcycle burns across boundaries, transcending language and culture. It has, in fact, become an entire culture in itself.

King of the Customizers

Arlen Ness and his wife Bev opened their first store in San Leandro, California in 1970. Almost 30 years later, Arlen reigns as the undisputed king of custom Harleys.

In many ways, his history runs parallel to the history of customizing. Arlen built his early reputation on innovative paint jobs. The small store was only open in the evenings and functioned primarily as a way to stop customers from constantly coming to his house to drop off or pick up parts. One of Arlen's big turning points came when he created a unique set of "ram horn" handlebars for his own bike. The bars were a great success and soon Arlen and Bev had people lined up outside the store to buy a set of Arlen Ness handlebars.

Arlen Ness became part of the motorcycle aftermarket, providing would-be customizers with the unique parts necessary to build a custom bike of their own. As time went by, Arlen added more handlebar designs, struts to replace the shock absorbers, complete springer fork assemblies, and various sheet metal parts.

Ten years later, Arlen and Bev moved to a larger store. It is interesting to note that during the time the custom Harley market was sliding into the doldrums, Arlen continued to build bikes for both himself and his customers. While many shops were closing or scaling back their operations, Arlen was able to show modest growth.

Left **After more than 30 years as a prolific bike builder, Arlen Ness never seems to run out of new ideas.**

Above **Arlen's Ferrari bike is another of his larger-than-life motorcycles. A massive 128 ci (2,098 cc) V-twin force fed by two superchargers and four carburetors.**

That growth left him well positioned when the world of custom Harleys started its renaissance in the early 1990s. The rebirth of the V-twin sent people scrambling for new ideas and parts. Many of those bikers and builders found the Arlen Ness store in San Leandro.

One visitor was the new owner of Drag Specialties. After being let down a hundred times by people who "evaluated" his parts by sending them to Taiwan for manufacture there, Arlen forged his first good relationship with a large aftermarket catalog company. Today all the major catalogs feature Arlen's parts, and every major magazine carries ads.

The bikes

A Knucklehead was Arlen's first ride and first custom Harley, but during the early years of the 1970s he built many Sportsters as well. Most of these bikes contained a new front frame section, fork, and sheet metal. When Arlen was finished, very little of the original bike remained. Never afraid to go his own way, Arlen turned away from the super-long choppers of the day and started building bikes that were low and lean, "diggers" in the slang of the day.

Ness bikes have always had a certain style, a look all their own, as well as a host of mechanical innovations. With help from chassis builder Jim Davis, Arlen was able to create long frames from small-diameter chrome-moly tubing. Sheet metal fabricator Bob Monroe helped Arlen create his own unique fenders and gas tanks, often with hidden oil tanks that routed the oil through the frame instead of through conventional oil lines.

In 1979, Arlen's newest bike, Two Bad, debuted in the custom bike magazines. Built around two Sportster engines set in a Jim Davis fabricated frame, Two Bad forever set Arlen apart from the other bike customizers of the day. Throughout the 1980s Arlen continued to produce wonderful works of mechanical art, including his Blown Shovelhead and Nesstique, a Sportster with antique styling.

If Nesstique looked old and spindly, Arlen's Ferrari Bike looked modern, fast, and massive. Another of Arlen's major bikes, the Ferrari machine, utilized two blowers, four carburetors, and Testarossa styling cues.

One of Arlen's major strengths is his ability to shift gears in a design sense. After building the sleek and flowing Ferrari bike, he decided to build a chopper complete with a wild overlapping flamed paint job. The first chopper was so well received that Arlen continues to build a few each year. Some have the old Panhead engine, while others have the Shovelhead or Evolution engines.

If Arlen was one of the first to turn away from the super-long choppers, he was also the first to embrace the idea of rubber mounting the engine. Arlen pioneered the long-low-cafe look for FXR Model Harley-Davidsons when they first came out and went on to build his own rubber-mount chassis. The very popular Luxury Liners are based on his second generation rubber-mount chassis.

He's also built a few early-style Sportsters in his own frame. Of course, there are also those other stray bikes, like the long red Aero bike that looks like it should be in a museum, the Bugatti bike he built some years ago, the aluminum bike with the overhead camshaft motor, and plans for a dozen more.

Arlen Ness never stops building and creating motorcycles, and each one is more interesting than the last.

***Left* This Arlen Ness chopper, like all good choppers, rides on a hardtail frame and uses a springer fork up front. And like an early chopper this one comes without any additional rake or an extended fork.**

The Others in the Business

No doubt Arlen Ness is the king of customizing. But there are others in the business who have left their indelible mark on this unique field with their innovative, and sometimes radical, designs.

Donnie Smith

Fans of Donnie Smith may not be surprised to learn that one of our best-known customizers started life on a farm in rural Minnesota. Today, Donnie acknowledges this agricultural upbringing as the environment in which he learned his basic mechanical skills. His natural ability to fix things like a broken combine was enhanced when he was sent to a high school which specialized in farming and machine maintenance.

It was after high school and a stint in the army that Donnie's natural talent for machines led him to the local drag strip outside his new home of Minneapolis, Minnesota. Donnie soon found himself part of a successful drag racing team campaigning at Willy's Gasser. By 1971 Donnie and his racing partners were earning a good living from tuning and fabrication work.

The first Smith Brothers and Fetrow shop was designed as a place to build complete cars for other racers, and thus help the three partners pay for their own drag racing habit. The first motorcycle work was done simply as a favor to a friend. Within a few years motorcycles and motorcycle-related projects occupied all the space in the shop. Eventually the race car had to go, in order to make way for even more motorcycles.

In the slang of the times, Smith Brothers and Fetrow was a chopper

Left **Part mechanic and part artist, Donnie Smith combines his strong mechanical background with a good sense of proportion and design.**

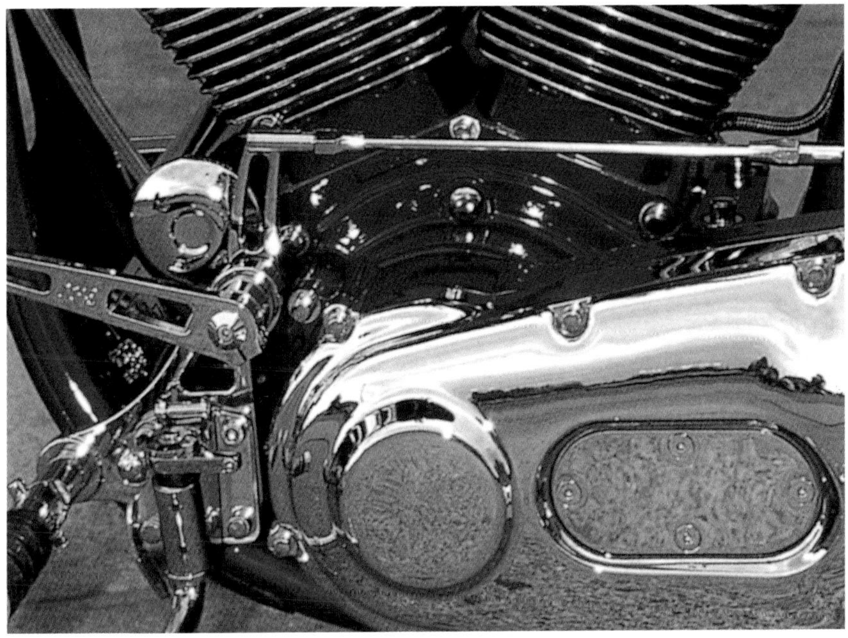

shop, and a very successful one at that. Many of those Donnie Smith designed frames, forks, and smaller pieces were manufactured in the shop, and then sold through custom outlets all over the country.

When the modified motorcycle market went soft in the mid-1980s, Donnie and his two partners decided to close the business. After taking a break, Donnie gravitated into the small garage at his house. With a bit of work the garage became a workshop and various one-off bikes began to roll out of the front door.

Above **Donnie Smith billet coil bracket, with ignition switch and painted coil covers. Forward controls are from AMS.**

Today, Donnie manages a crew of four and a constantly ringing telephone in a fairly large commercial building located in Blaine, Minnesota. Bike projects range from simple rake and stretch jobs, to complete turn-key bikes. At any one time there are at least two bikes mocked-up and waiting for sheet metal pieces, and another one or two undergoing final assembly.

Donnie's relatively new relationship with Chrome Specialties, as a designer and builder for in-house products, means more work of all kinds for the shop. The heavy workload and frequent travel to events makes for a very busy Donnie Smith. Sometimes, especially during busy times of the year, the hours get rather long. To watch him move about the shop, encouraging the lead mechanic, then discussing the shape of a fender with his fabricator, before taking another phone call, it's difficult to imagine Donnie Smith doing anything else.

Dave Perewitz

Dave Perewitz seems like a pretty happy-go-lucky person. At events he always seems to be laughing and telling jokes, the loud Boston accent carrying across the room. Yet, underneath that jovial

exterior is a thoughtful custom bike builder, dedicated to producing stylish Harleys.

Dave's first foray into professional Harley-Davidson painting and repair came early, when he put up a small shop behind his father's house in the early 1970s. With help from his brother Donnie, Dave was able to paint and build a number of custom bikes each year, some of which found their way into the custom magazines.

Ten years later Dave and Donnie were still at it, building and painting motorcycles and forming friendships with other builders like Arlen Ness, Donnie Smith, and Don Hotop. By the early 1980s, David had a larger shop and a separate retail store in Brockton, Massachusetts. As the business grew David's wife Susan helped by keeping the books.

Today, David still owns the store in Brockton and he still does most of the fabrication and paint work at a separate shop close to the house. What has changed is the nature of the work and who he works for. No longer do the new fabricated parts simply go onto a customer's bike and out of the door. Innovative designs turn into retail parts sold through his evolving relationship with Sullivan Brothers, or occasionally, Nempco.

What hasn't changed over the years is David's immense ability to design and produce great-looking custom motorcycles. His style has evolved with the times, yet you can usually tell a Perewitz bike by the exceptional paint and the extraordinary way the whole motorcycle hangs together as a design, and not just as a collection of nice parts.

Above **As much a designer as builder, Dave Perewitz has a knack for building bikes that stylistically flow from one end to the other.**

Left **Dave Perewitz likes his tanks long and concave on the bottom, separated by a smooth dash without any gauges.**

Mild to Wild

Harley-Davidson customized bikes in every size, shape, and color imaginable. From 54 ci (883 cc) sportsters to monster-motor Softails. From bikes that rely on aftermarket frames to those that use a stock FXR chassis. Because of the enormous variety of Harley-Davidson customs, the machines don't always fit into neat categories. Elsewhere this book is grouped logically, but this chapter is for machines that didn't fit elsewhere – like the Softail with so much one-off equipment that it doesn't fit in the Softail chapter, and the two FXR bikes that we've called a mild custom instead of rubber-mount bikes. Or the Arlen Ness bike with the overhead cam engine that uses an FXR-style rubber-mounting system. Or the European bikes: neither is a Softail and both bolt the engine rigidly to the frame. You get the idea. Think of this chapter as a variety pack with a tasty new surprise on every page!

An FXR Built to Boogie

Model used: 1988 FXR

The makeover: The sheet metal, the motor, and transmission were stripped. The FXR was reduced to a bare frame surrounded by fenders, wheels, and assorted parts.

The bottom end of the 80 ci (1,311 cc) V-twin was rebuilt and balanced by Jim Thompson from Dedham, Massachusetts. The Harley heads were then ported, and new black diamond valves and Jim Thompson valve springs were installed. South Shore Plating polished the cylinders and heads before Auto Tec painted the cases and the areas between the fins.

With the cases and bottom end finished, a stout EV 59 Camshaft from Andrews with 0.560 in. (1.4 cm) of lift was installed. Then, new high-compression Wiseco pistons were installed, followed by the polished and painted "ten-over" cylinders. The ported heads and adjustable push rods were next, topped off with chrome-plated Sportster rocker boxes. Near the end of the engine project the polished Mikuni carburetor, Compu-fire ignition, and Perewitz/Sullivan billet coil bracket and coils were added.

The 5-speed transmission was completely dissembled and the stock gears replaced with back-cut cogs from Andrews. Externally, the transmission was treated much like the engine, with a painted case and a billet Perewitz top cover.

The factory-made 39 mm narrow-glide forks have been rebuilt with new seals, Works springs, and damper tubes from Progressive Suspension. A pair of Koni shocks, 1 in. (2.5 cm) lower than stock provide good handling and bring the back end of the bike down to match the height of the front. The frame itself is nearly stock. A modest wedge-rake was done and 5 degrees were added to the fork angle. All the rough areas on the frame were then molded.

The deep red paint seen on the new ride is kandy brandywine from House of Kolor. Nancy Brooks did the simple silver graphics, which are buried under a series of clearcoats.

For brakes, GMA 4-piston calipers and master cylinders were chosen, with one in the front and another at the back. The rest of the wheel and brake hardware comes from the Sullivan/Perewitz partnership.

The polished rotors and rear belt pulley all match the design of the Desperado billet wheels. The rear wheel measures 16 in. (41 cm) and carries a 140 series Avon tire. The front tire, this one stamped 90/90x19, surrounds a Desperado billet wheel. The sheet metal is very similar to the stock sheet metal that had subsequently been taken off, with the addition of a Sportster taillight molded into the back fender.

Below **The taillight is an early Harley light molded into the fender. Stock swingarm uses upgraded aftermarket hardware for the axle mounting, adjusting, and the pivots.**

Good Parts Make a Great Motorcycle

Model used: FXR

The makeover: Once apart, the FXR frame received a mild rake job, but no additional stretch. Seven additional degrees seemed plenty, just enough to place the front wheel in front of the bike.

The rest of the changes made to the frame are more subtle. The area under the seat, the signature triangular area, contains a number of small changes. Under the side covers, the triangle has been paneled in. The side covers themselves look stock at first, until you take a second look. The two side covers for each side were taken and one longer cover was made. Normally the covers fit inside the tubes; but these new ones reach out and overlap the tubes slightly. This makes that area seem a little longer than usual. It also stretches out the whole bike.

Another change is the oil tank. The standard FXR tank extends out from under the seat until it almost reaches the rear cylinder. By crafting a taller oil tank with the same capacity, but no bulge, this area is opened up to give the bike a lighter feel. Other frame work includes the addition of new shock absorber mounting points on the stock swingarm.

Like the frame changes, most of the stock sheet metal was massaged and used again. The front fender is minus the rivets that used to hold it together and the gas tank, with the small Donnie Smith gas cap, fits the frame much better than did the original. At the back, the early-style taillight is now an integral part of the fender and the license plate sits on a slanted bracket above the taillight. The only totally new piece of sheet metal is the small air dam located behind the front wheel. This adds a truly nice accent created by Rob Roehl.

The chassis hardware is a combination of modified Harley-Davidson parts and high-grade components from the aftermarket. The stock Showa fork with the 39 mm forks is still there, holding up the front wheel, though now the frame sits 2 in. (5 cm) lower than it did before. What didn't come from Harley-Davidson is the 4-piston

calipers with the PM logo milled into their surface, or the floating rotors on either side of the Sturgis 19 in. (48 cm) aluminum wheel.

Brake and wheel hardware at the back matches that used in front, though, of course, the wheel measures 16 in. (41 cm) in diameter and mounts a 150 series Avon tire that was somehow squeezed into the space normally filled by a 130 tire – which was a feat in itself.

The engine follows the same theme, a combination of modified

Above **Deep purple used on cases and cylinders complements the magenta paint seen on the sheet metal. Even the inner primary, coils, and the center part of the rocker boxes are painted in the purple hue.**

original parts and very high quality aftermarket components. Local engine builder Lee Wickstrom completely disassembled the engine and then sent the cases and cylinders out for polishing and powder coating. The stock flywheel assembly was then balanced, and the lower end reassembled with new bearings. Next, the Harley cylinders were

Left **This FXR exhibits a certain synergy. The basically good design is enhanced through a long series of seemingly minor changes and upgrades.**

filled with S&S high-compression pistons, topped off with complete S&S cylinder heads.

A 561 camshaft and the Super G carburetor, both from S&S, are recommended. To round out the breathing part of the engine package, a set of Python pipes from Drag Specialties was chosen.

The 5-speed transmission is filled with back-cut gears for easier shifting; all housed in a polished case with a chrome top cover and a billet ART side cover that houses the hydraulic slave cylinder.

The magenta paint from House of Kolor is the work of Jerry Scherer while the subtle graphics are by Craig Smith. The rest of the hardware continues the quality theme seen throughout the bike: Arlen Ness bars with billet grips and a small speedo and tachometer from Drag Specialties.

A good engine makes power because all parts work together in mechanical harmony. Likewise, a nice custom motorcycle achieves its appeal, not because of one part, but because all the parts and pieces work to create a certain visual impact. Together, Clayton Shepard, Donnie Smith, and all the rest involved in this project, used the good parts to build a great motorcycle.

No Regard for Borders

Model used: FXE

The makeover: First, the front of the frame was cleaned up and all the factory welds molded. The one-piece gas tank with twin fillers is a Battistini original, as are the elaborate louvered side covers that enclose the oil tank and extend down to the frame and back to the shock absorbers.

The taildragger rear fender is from Arlen Ness, as are the flamed grips and billet floorboards.

The wheels, measuring 21 in. (53 cm) in front and 18 in. (46 cm) at the back, are from another well-known American company, Performance Machine, as are the 4-piston calipers used on both the front and rear of the bike. An extremely short pair of reservoir shock absorbers connects the twin rail Arlen Ness swing arm to the Harley's frame.

Up front the suspension comes by way of the Paughco chrome-plated springer fork assembly. And apparently, a bike with a springer fork needs ape-hanger bars.

Outside, the cases, cylinders, and heads received a thorough polishing job. Inside, the cylinders received a

Right **A traditional bike with Shovelhead engine, springer fork, and ape-hanger bars, with innovative side covers, billet wheels, and even billet floorboards.** ***Horst Rösler.***

clean-up bore and new Harley pistons, new bearings for the bottom end, and new valves for the Shovelheads. A Crane cam opens the valves while a Series E carburetor from S&S mixes the fuel. Exhaust is handled by the wild upswept pipes from Custom Chrome.

The stock 4-speed transmission bolts to the frame just behind the engine, though it too received the polish, paint, and rebuild routine used for the engine. A primary belt connects engine and transmission, hidden behind the ribbed and polished aluminum primary cover.

The very complex paint job with overlapping flames is the work of an American painter, Jeff McCann. Jeff used lacquer paints from House of Kolor to create the tangerine layout with lime green flames and fuchsia highlights.

An Arlen Ness air cleaner, FuB forward controls, and hand made switch panel for the left side, round out the parts and accessories used to complete the final assembly of this international creation.

Left **18 in. (46 cm) PM rim is supported by the Arlen Ness swingarm. Shovelheads were built in the days when most bikes used chain drive to the rear wheel. The fabricated chain guard matches the design of the switch panel.** ***Horst Rösler.***

Right **Not many of the original Shovelheads came with an air cleaner like this one. Note the cam cover and the flamed kick start lever.**

French Finesse For a German Custom

Model used: FXR

The makeover: Built by the Legend bike shop in Schellebelle, Belgium, this Orange Evo-powered custom combines the best attributes of both German and French bike builders.

The hot engine in this Legendary bike comes from a 97 ci (1,590 cc) engine based on Sputhe cases and cylinders capped by Edelbrock heads. Inside the polished cases and cylinders is an S&S 4.25 in. (3 cm) flywheel assembly and 3 in. (8 cm) Sputhe pistons. Gas and air enter the big bore brute via a Mikuni carburetor each time the Crane cam opens an intake valve. Spark comes with help from a Crane HI-4 ignition, and the spent gas and air exit via the Carbon Dream pipes.

A stock primary chain takes the power of the Sputhe engine to a set of 5-speed gears housed in a Softail-style transmission. Even though the bike is not a Softail, the engine and transmission mount to the frame directly, as they do in a Softail (unlike bikes with "rubber-mount" engines).

Right **This machine combines a large displacement V-twin with an aftermarket frame and sheet metal.** ***Horst Rösler.***

The frame from Custom Framesale in Holland is manufactured from mild steeltubing with 5 in. (13 cm) of stretch and a 36-degree fork angle. The fork itself is a high-performance upside down design from W.P. in Holland, supporting a 3-spoke aluminum wheel. The wheels used on this bike are an interesting choice for two reasons. First, they measure 17 in. (43 cm) in diameter, an uncommon size for a Harley custom. Second, they come not from the aftermarket, but from a Suzuki sport bike.

The twin 4-piston brake calipers used at the front come from the same Suzuki, as does the single caliper and

Left **Front and rear brakes come from a donor Suzuki, mounted here with a fabricated bracket.**

Right **Sputhe cylinders and engine cases are made from their own Nitralloy aluminum alloy for maximum strength. Cylinders are cast around a steel liner so it becomes an integral part of the cylinders.**

Above **Massive swingarm is built to accommodate a wide 190x17 in. (483x43 cm) tire, but something had to give – there is no room for belt drive.**

rotor combination used on the rear wheel. And while some modern Harleys use belt final drive, this one uses a chain between the transmission and rear wheel, to make room for the 190/80x17 in. (483/203x43 cm) Metzeler rear tire.

The rear wheel is supported by the fabricated swingarm machined from a solid piece of 6061 aluminum. The same raw material is used for the unique rear fender struts and the bracket used to support the carbon fiber muffler.

Custom Framesale supplied the very modern front fender and the more traditional rear fender. They also fabricated a one-piece gas tank and the custom-fit oil tank located just below the seat. The paint color is midnight orange, sprayed in acrylic lacquer, with airbrush graphics applied on top of the orange and then buried under a series of clearcoats.

Though the bike contains very few parts that are actually from Harley-Davidson, it is, indeed, a very colorful custom Harley.

A 'Cammer' from Arlen

Model used: V-twin

The makeover: The idea of placing the camshafts above the valves isn't new. Racing motorcycles and cars have used single and double overhead cams for more than 30 years.

However, this technology was never before applied to the standard Harley Big Twin engine. Enter Arlen Ness, who by chance met an innovative machinist, a man who had already designed several overhead camshaft kits for the small-block Chevy V-8. It didn't take long for Arlen to ask if a similar conversion could be done for the all American V-twin.

The design dispenses with the conventional cam, pushrods, lifters, rocker arms, and rocker boxes. Instead, a single camshaft, supported by an aluminum housing, bolts onto each head. In addition to the camshaft, each of these housings contains two roller rocker arms supported by their own shafts. A crank-driven gear, located where the camshaft once lived, turns the two camshafts through a toothed belt.

In a standard pushrod engine the valve springs have to close the valve, as the cam lobe rolls past the high point. In doing so, they have to work against the inertia of all the valve-train parts. Pushrods and tappets get heavy at high RPM, especially on an engine with long pushrods and relatively large roller tappets.

Left **The unusual form assembly allow Arlen to raise or lower the front of the bike without disassembling the fork. Note the large diameter rotors and Arlen Ness calipers.**

Because the new overhead cam design eliminates most of those heavy valve-train parts, the heads can be assembled with lighter valve springs.

With the new valve gear the engines revved much more quickly and easily, though the redline had to remain rather conservative due to the basic internal dimensions of a stock V-twin. With a bore of 3.5 in. (9 cm) and a stroke of 4.25 in. (12 cm) these are never going to be 7,000 RPM engines, no matter how sophisticated the valve gear is.

Arlen thought it would be interesting to bolt the overhead cam kit onto an engine with different bore and stroke dimensions, one that could take better advantage of the overhead design. A discussion with S&S produced an engine based on a set of their big-bore cases designed for a 4 in. (10 cm) bore. By mating these to a crankshaft with a 4 in. (10 cm) stroke, they created a "square" engine.

Above **Normally the boring side of a V-twin engine, you can see how the front exhaust pipe makes a U-turn to run across the left side of the polished and painted cylinders. The vertical member behind the seat and tubes that form the seat areas have been radically altered to get the seat so low.**

Right **More than just a custom motorcycle with an innovative engine, Arlen's red Racer is a bike built on new ideas. Note the fenders, headlight, air dam, gas tank, and exhaust pipes.**

A special engine needs a special chassis. In this case, it's an Arlen Ness FXR-style chassis with some serious modifications. First, the frame is modified near the back to dramatically drop the seat height. Instead of using one of his standard dual-rail swingers, Arlen put together a triangulated swingarm that looks like something from a radical Softail-style chassis.The shock absorbers are supported by the frame immediately behind the seat, making for an almost horizontal mounting position. The special shock absorbers are from Fournales, and use high-pressure air in place of the standard spring.

The unusual swingarm leaves room for a 180x18 in. (457x46 cm) Metzeler tire and belt drive. Mounted outboard of the drive pulley is the large-diameter brake rotor and below that the 4-piston brake caliper.

The front fork assembly uses sliding axle supports so the ride height is adjustable over a wide range. The tubes themselves mount to radiused billet mid-glide triple trees. Dual disk brakes with new 6-piston calipers slow down the front wheel, which is covered by a very brief fender with billet supports. The rear fender is bobbed, much like the front, and uses similar aluminum supports.

Though the exhaust pipes run down the right side in typical fashion, the routing is rather unique. The pipe

for the front cylinderhead makes a sharp left turn and runs across the left side of the engine before crossing over again to run side by side with the other pipe. The unique routing prevents any kind of interference between the pipe and the trick drive system for the overhead camshafts.

Arlen's long time friend, The Mun, did much of the fabrication on this bike, including the turn-down gas tank and the unusual front-air dam. The molding on the frame and sheet metal parts is the work of Jesse Diaz while the paint and graphics come from Brouhad Design.

Off the Scale

Model used: Softail

The makeover: Some bikes are nice, some are awesome, and a very few are off the scale. The red Softail seen here definitely falls into the off the scale category.

Built by Jesse James, owner of West Coast Choppers, the red bike catches your eye when first seen from across the parking lot at a crowded event. The frame was built in-house. Instead of using solid steel vertical side plates under the seat, Jesse used concave half tubing bent into a curve. The rear fender is supported by similar material, which arches and tapers as it runs to the end of the fender. It's an unusual bike, and one has to wonder just how it was created.

Gordon Rooth, a fabricator in Jesse's shop, started with two of their own blanks to create the tapered rear fender and the very trim and graceful front fender. The gas tank is Jesse's own. He fabricated the whole thing

Right **The unique air cleaner, gas tank, and exhaust pipes were all fabricated for this one machine.**

Below **The Fender Man, Jesse James, a man on his way up.**

Above **Nearly all the parts on Jesse's new bike were fabricated by hand. To describe this as a softail-style custom doesn't really do it justice.**

from scratch using only a sheet of raw aluminum.

The unusual wheels are one-off designs, carved on a very large CNC machine from a big chunk of billet aluminum, big enough that the rims are an integral part of the spokes. The front rim measures 19 in (48 cm) in diameter and relies on a really slim, trim Jesse James fork assembly for support. At the back a 180x18 in. (457x46 cm) Metzeler wraps a matching rim and spoke combination. A single 4-piston Performance Machine brake caliper mounts at either end. The rotors are two more Jesse James originals.

The only piece Jesse didn't fabricate is the polished V-twin, though even that is almost a one-off piece. The cases and 4.25 in. (11 cm) S&S flywheel assembly might be common enough, but the 3.5 in.

(9 cm) Patrick Racing billet cylinders and matching heads aren't what you would call commonplace. The hand formed aluminum air cleaner protects a Super G carburetor from S&S, while a pair of fabricated exhaust pipes run down along the bottom frame rail.

Damon's Painting applied the red hue to the frame, fenders, tank, and the headlight shell. Koon did most of the final assembly, including running the wiring inside the frame, and installation of the fabricated bars and grips.

Below **Low profile 18 in. tires used on both ends work well with the overall design. One-off wheels exhibit a great shape, matched by the brake rotors.**

Customized Xs...

As the world around us changes it is reassuring to consider the Sportster. First introduced in 1957 as the XL, the Sportster still carries the same name and even the same essential look that it did over forty years ago.

Introduced originally as a "sporty" Harley-Davidson, it went from early super bike to cheap Harley, to a woman's bike, but recently it seems to be returning with more of that original sporty intent. Through it all, the original design has remained intact. Though there are hundreds of thousands of Sportsters on the street, a really nice customized Sportster still seems a rarity.

Presented here is an overview of street bikes – from a fabricated Cafe racer to a light touring machine. From a German road racer to a modernized late model Sportster. Because they are uncommon, these Sportsters take on special significance. These aren't just customized Harleys, these are customized Harley-Davidson Sportsters.

A Bike of Her Own

Model: Sportster

The Sportster's new skirted front fender and Fat Bob-style tank came from the Custom Chrome catalog, and both are designed to fit the late-model Sportster chassis.

Most of the work on the bike was done by Marty and the crew at the Sport Center. For the paint work, however, the sheet metal was sent to Scott McTavish at Gene's Auto Body in Duluth, Minnesota. Scott used Harley-Davidson paint, a candy red on top, and birch white on the lower part of the gas tank.

The new gas tank obviously meant a new speedometer. The crew at the Sport Center installed a Harley-Davidson speedometer and ignition switch. The mini light bar used to relocate the rear turn signals is from Custom Chrome, however, as is the lay-down license plate bracket. A fringed solo seat from Mike Corbin replaced the stock seat. To make sure there would be room to stretch out on the highway a set of forward controls from Custom Chrome were added.

Some of the changes are more subtle than the sheet metal, though no less important in the long run. The large front turn signals, for example, were discarded and replaced by unobtrusive oval accessory lights mounted just below the switch assembly on either side. In order to provide some storage space, a pair of Harley-Davidson leather saddle bags were added to the rear. The combination of Fat Bob-style tank, saddle bags, and two-tone paint scheme all work to give the Sportster the look of an early big twin.

Left **The paint job was borrowed from an older Harley catalog. The logo is also older, from the early 1960s. Many parts like this are still available from the dealers.**

Above **In the wind: Jean on her first customized bike.**

To really lock in that look of a bigger bike from an earlier period, a few more accents were added. At the front, for example, there's the chrome-plated engine guard. Between the cylinders on the left side is the antique style horn from Harley-Davidson. And in place of the stock rectangular mirrors are the round mirrors, also from Harley-Davidson.

You can hardly have a custom Harley these days without having it lowered. In this bike a pair of shortened shocks bring the rear end down a full two inches. The front fork was shortened by the same amount, with a factory low-suspension fork kit.

When it came to the engine, turn-out mufflers were chosen. The rest of the bike was left alone.

The Ability to See

Model: Sportster

The Sportster in this case was stripped down to its bare bones. The bike surgery included not only the neck and swingarm, but also the more subtle work done for cosmetic reasons.

In order to run a wider rear tire, an FXR rear fender, modified here to accept a '41 Chevy Taillight, was suggested and was supported by fabricated struts. Instead of a Sportster gas tank, a Sport Bob tank from a company in California was recommended. Though the tank came with two gas caps there was only one, placed in the center, when the tank was finished. The final piece of cosmetic work came in the form of a one-piece battery and ignition cover for the left side.

All lingering scars were eliminated and a careful "plastic surgery" was carried out to give the frame its clean lines, and the tank and fenders their smooth surface. With the plastic work finished, the single-stage metallic green paint was applied. The final clearcoats were given after the graphics were done.

The engine already displaced 73 ci (1,200 cc) and breathed through heads

Right **Not a radical ride, but a long way from the original cafe-Sportster.**

with enlarged valves, so Lee Wickstrom from Kokesh M-C only needed to install a new crankshaft assembly and a set of Andrews V4 camshafts. The Super E carb that came with the bike was left in place, while a pair of Python pipes were added as a good compromise between traditional looks and good performance.

While the engine was still apart, its covers were sent out for chrome plating. All except the center rings of the rocker box set, which were painted green to match the rest of

the machine. During the disassembly the cylinders were painted black, though the heads were bead blasted and left in raw aluminum to give them a shiny appearance.

Left **The aftermarket tank has been converted to a single filler with a slightly raised rib along the top.**

Below **By enclosing the battery and ignition module under one fabricated cover, the bike takes on cleaner lines.**

Another of the little improvements is the spoked wheels used in place of the cast originals. Gary at Kokesh M-C laced up the 19 in. (48 cm) front and 16 in. (41 cm) wheels with chrome rims and twisted spokes for extra sparkle.

The seat is from Keith Nybo, built on the seat pan supplied by Donnie Smith. The stretched swingarm of the new seat mounts farther back than the original and provides more room to stretch out arms and legs.

A Flat Track XR Built For the Street

Model: XR 1000

It all started with an XR 1000 motor purchased by Larry Page during Bike Week at Daytona.

The next step was to give it a frame. In this instance a frame in the form of a late model Sportster frame that had been used but was otherwise sound.

A motor and a frame may be the essence of a motorcycle, but that isn't enough to have a running XR 1000.

The motor was shipped to Departure Bike Works in Richmond, Virginia, where it was pulled apart for a complete inspection. The heads had already received some port work, and everything else looked to be in good shape. Departure's job then was to freshen the internals and brighten the

Left **From this angle it's easy to see the Sportster in this XR.**

Above **Storz supplied the SuperTrapp exhaust for the left side, as well as the dirt track-inspired gas tank.**

externals with polished covers and heads, and stainless-steel fasteners.

To complete the chassis, a (43 mm) Ceriani fork assembly from Storz and a pair of short, Progressive shock absorbers for the rear were bought. A Storz one-piece gas tank became the perfect choice for this competition-inspired XR. Harder to find was the special oil tank, with the recess to clear the rear carburetor. A factory tank was finally located on a dealer's shelf.

Next, the old Sportster frame was cleaned up and repaired. The frame with stock rake and stretch dimensions was left, but the short stubby tubes at the very back of the frame were modified. Instead of mounting the fender strut, the frame stub was trimmed and extended to blend into the fender and support it without the need for a strut. To eliminate those ugly bolt heads, the new un-strut was tapped so the fender bolts could be screwed in from the backside.

For the other end of the frame a pair of mid-glide trees from 6061 aluminum were fabricated. In keeping with the performance theme, a pair of 4-piston calipers from PM were bolted to the front lower legs. At the back, another PM, 4-piston caliper squeezes a ventilated, polished rotor.

Left **In the best racing tradition this bike uses a Ceriani 43-mm fork assembly, dual four-piston Performance Machine brake calipers, and a very trim front fender.**

Rather than using the more traditional 19 and 16 in. (48 cm and 41 cm) wheels and tires, this XR carries 18 in. (46 cm) Avon rubber at both ends. The Avon tires mount on light 18 in. (46 cm) aluminum wheels from Performance Machine.

The Storz-supplied flat-track gas tank forms the center piece of the simplified sheet metal for the modified XR. The minimalist fenders, fabricated by Milwaukee Iron, might not keep off much rain, but the style fits the rest of this bare-bones bike. At the very back an early-style Harley-Davidson taillight is molded into the fender itself. The solo seat is another one-off item, this time from the able hands of Danny Gray. When all the parts were finished, the frame and sheet metal were shipped to Keith Saunders for the bright orange and white paint job.

For an exhaust system a set of SuperTrapp pipes from Storz were used. The handlebars are flat-track style with just a little lift and integral risers. Instead of being rear-set, the brake and shift levers are located in their standard Sportster location for easier around-town riding.

A Street Legal Road Racer

Model: XR 1000

The Milwaukee Racing Center, located in Oberthal, Germany, is in the business of transforming stock Harleys into more aggressive, powerful, and roadworthy motorcycles.

Hans Jürgen Boujong, owner of the Race Center, sells the full line of parts from WiWo, a well-known German company that designs and sells high-performance parts for both race track and street use.

Hans and crew built a bike that definitely puts the Sport back in Sportster. While the low and slow crowd slam their Big Twins right to the ground for boulevard cruising or stoplight racing, this Sportster sits high and dry to maximize clearance on corners.

The stock rear shocks (due to be replaced with some high-quality aftermarket shocks) bolt to the rather substantial WiWo swingarm with the eccentric axle adjusters. The adjusters are used to tension the belt that runs to the rear pulley. The pulley itself bolts to an innovative WiWo disk wheel. The modular design allows the owner to change the rim at a later date, without buying an entire new wheel and hub assembly. The wheel in question is 17 in. (43 cm) in diameter, matched to a 3.5 in. (9 cm) rim, wide enough to support the Bridgestone 140x17 in. tire.

The front suspension is equally "normal". The WiWo inverted front fork uses air in place of springs to support the bike. Aluminum triple trees, again from WiWo, mount the fork assembly to the frame. The disk-style front wheel bolts to an aluminum rim with an 18 in.

Left **We always think of motorcycles and their riders in groups, yet the motorcycle provides a solitary experience.** ***Horst Rösler.***

Left **Stock Sportster tanks aren't known for their capacity. This Quick Bob tank holds more gas and gives the bike a very different look.**

Below Left **The WiWo wheels have a number of advantages; light weight and high strength are primary. The owner can change rim sizes without changing hub or disk.**

Below Right **The SuperTrapp mufflers are tunable, both the noise level and the engine's output can be modified according to how many disks are used.**

(46 cm) diameter coupled with a Bridgestone tire.

The brakes for this street-legal road racer are made up of standard, high-performance components, like the single WiWo 4-piston caliper and 13 in. (330 mm) rotor used on the front wheel. The somewhat less important rear brake uses another 4-piston caliper mated to a smaller, 9 in. (230 mm) rotor.

Hans considered the performance of the 73 ci (1,200 cc) Sportster engine to be more than adequate,

Right **The German-built Sportster sits high, the better to allow plenty of clearance when carving through the countryside at high speed.** ***Horst Rösler.***

and replaced only the carburetor with a Series E from S&S, and the exhaust with the dirt track pipes from SuperTrapp.

Though the emphasis here is on the hardware and parts that make the machine a more precise two-wheeled bullet, the not-so-hard components are also interesting. The front fender, for example, is a collaboration between Hans and the people at WiWo. The trim shape is made from carbon fiber to be both light and durable. The gas tank is from Zodiac, a Fat Bob design intended to fit Sportster frames. And finally, the rear fender and seat combination comes from the crew at the Racing Center.

Relatively flat Sportster bars on short risers point the way, with both speedometer and tachometer mounted dead center to tell you how fast you're going. Grips on both ends, and the mirrors, are all from Arlen Ness. The rear-set brake and shift levers provide the proper Cafe seating position.

The Milwaukee Racing Center managed to build a faster, more corner-friendly motorcycle.

Not Just Another "CR"

Model: XLCR Sportster

In 1977 Harley-Davidson introduced a radical new model, the XLCR Sportster. The "CR" stood for Cafe Racer and the model came with an extended tank, small fairing, and abbreviated rear fender.

At the time of its introduction the bike was seen as too different, and despite Willie G's best intentions, sales of the new Cafe racer were very disappointing. Now, more than 20 years after its introduction, the XLCR has gone from ugly duckling to collectible classic.

In this case, a 1977 Sportster was first disassembled completely. Then, the frame was stretched 4 in. (10 cm) and the neck raked an additional five degrees. With the top tube extended, it was time to bolt on a genuine XLCR gas tank – an essential part of the conversion to Sportster CR. Rather than try to find a factory tail section, an old fiberglass chopper fender and "night light" taillight assembly was found. The look is similar to that of a factory CR, yet unique to this motorcycle.

Right **This bike is a combination of off-the-shelf parts and hand-fabricated hardware. Front fairing and fender are from Arlen Ness and gas tank is from Harley Davidson.**

At the front of the bike a cafe-style fairing and a small fender from the Arlen Ness catalog were used, to mimic the look of the factory CRs. Mounted inside the fairing is a simple gauge set with tachometer and speedo, both from Drag Specialties.

Even after finding and modifying most of the sheet metal, there were still plenty of parts to find and modify. A 1979 Sportster swingarm made mounting disk brakes and a late-model cast wheel easy. That meant moving the lower shock

mount forward to match the shock mounting on the earlier frame. The shocks themselves are shorter than stock, to lower the back of the bike roughly 3 in. (7.6 cm). While they were doing all this work the swingarm was "bridged" for strength and then sent off to the chrome-plating shop.

The front suspension is based on the original Sportster fork, cut by 2 in. (5 cm). The small PM calipers are mounted to the fender mounting points with special Donnie Smith brackets, with polished, drilled rotors.

The crew at Eagle Engineering of Minneapolis recommended more cubic inches, in the form of a stroker bottom end and a stock bore. This combination created a 74 ci (1,213 cc) street engine. To make the most of that, Eagle ported the Harley heads and installed four high-lift camshafts. Behind the classic S&S teardrop air filter sits an S&S Super E fuel mixer.

How the motor looks is almost as important as how it runs. The cases, cylinder fins, and heads were polished to a high luster. To create pipes similar to those used on the CR's, 1979 Sportster pipes were modified

Left **The unique gas tank is a factory CR item. This is actually the second tank. The first was mounted solid to the bike but developed cracks due to vibration.**

Below **The front halt of the exhaust is made up from a set of Sportster pipes combined with the double pipe fabricated section leading to the small collector.**

so they ran together from the point where they met to the single collector mounted on the right side.

The hand-fabricated oil tank, small chain guard, and bracket for the PM rear brake caliper are the work of Donnie Smith. For the custom seat, Keith Nybo was called on, while Rick Haugland did the great flamed paint job.

Bill's Little Project

Model: Evolution Sportster

The Makeover: Bill Mesenbrink took his wife's Evolution Sportster frame to versatile bike-builder Donnie Smith. The neck was raked an additional five degrees to give the bike a little more of what Donnie calls "attitude."

Donnie also created the one-piece battery and ignition cover on the left side. The rest of the sheet metal parts came from the Custom Chrome catalog, including the fenders and the Quick-Bob gas tank. The sheet metal parts and the gas tank, in particular, were designed to give the Sportster a bit of that Big Twin bulk.

Jon Kosmoski, of the House of Kolor fame, agreed to paint the bike and even the wheels, which involved a lot of extra taping.

Jon painted the sheet metal with kandy oriental blue sprayed over a blue metallic base. With design ideas provided by Patty Mesenbrink, he also painted the multicolored graphics and then buried everything under a series of clearcoats.

The original used Sportster was the base model – the one with the small engine, no radio, and no air conditioning. "Small" in this case is

Right **This unique paint design is by Jon Kosmoski. Details include polished factory wheels and chrome on the engine covers.**

a 54 ci (883 cc) V-twin that can best be described as an engine with a lot of potential.

The good news is the ease with which the small engine can be bored out and equipped with a 73 ci (1,200 cc) kit. At 73 ci (1,200 cc), most Sportster motors realize enough potential to give Big Twins a run for their money. Dewey's M.C. in Minneapolis bored out the cylinders to the new 73 ci (1,200 cc) dimension and also ported the heads to flow more air. Reassembly included a set

Left **Chrome plated lower legs are mounted in billet aluminum narrow-glide triple trees.**

Below Left **Although the engine looks as though it is powder coated, the purple is actually just plain old urethane paint .**

Below Right **Single speedometer and no tachometer. Handlebars with enough rise contribute to a nice comfortable seating position.**

of Andrews camshafts and a Crane HI-4 ignition. Along the way Bill took most of the engine parts over to his friend Frog's house where they carefully prepped the aluminum and applied the purple paint. The engine covers for both sides of the engine were re-chromed.

The 73 ci (1,200 cc) kit means more power, and embarrassment for the other bikes it rides with. The paint and unusual sheet metal mean lots of compliments.

S&S
SUPER

Hardtails — the Simplest

Hardtails have always been popular with a hardcore group of Harley enthusiasts. The first bobbers were built on a hardtail chassis, because that's all there was. Choppers, too, were built mostly with hardtail frames. Frames with shock absorbers were converted to hardtail-form by replacing the rear shocks with solid struts.

Hardtails bring riders back to the bare essentials of riding. Each hardtail contains two wheels, one engine, gas tank(s), and minimal controls. No rear suspension, no fancy dash, no full-coverage fenders.

They may be hard on your behind, and leave you with no room to pack a jacket, but that's the whole point. Without all the extras you're left with the real thing, an undiluted two-wheeled rush.

What follows is a look at five hardtails, all assembled in the past ten years. What all the bikes have in common is that certain hot rod flavor, a feeling that they were stripped down to go fast, and that essential spirit lives in all motorcycles, but is much easier to find in these very basic machines.

The Essential V-Twin Motorcycle

Model: Hardtail

If you ask Terry McConnell from Tulsa, Oklahoma, how he built the little silver hardtail, he makes it sound too easy.

Terry's account leaves out significant parts of the story. Things such as the sketches he did to ensure that the finished bike looked exactly like the idea he had in his mind. Or the careful selection of the right parts to achieve the correct finished effect.

In the case of this silver machine, Terry started with an idea for a simple bike, nice and light, with clean lines and no extra parts. A hardtail seemed the only answer, so Terry ordered a frame from Atlas with three inches of stretch and a 38-degree fork angle. During the mock-up stage a pair of fenders from Jesse James were clamped in place. The way the front fender wrapped close to the tire provided a certain appeal. At the back, a short fender was turned around and trimmed until it looked like it belonged on the emerging hardtail.

The wraparound side cover is the work of an outside fabricator, Steve Stonez from Stonez Bonez in Tulsa. Steve made the panel from sheet steel

Below **In the wind: Terry and Tina Mc Connell on their latest creation.**

according to the sketches, and also made the seat pan. For a gas tank, a stretched model from Fat Catz was chosen. The tank is listed as a model with a 5 in. (13 cm) stretch. You could mount it forward on the chassis and still have it come back far enough to meet the small custom seat.

Once the mocked-up bike was completed and studied, it all came apart one last time. The frame and sheet metal parts made their way to the paint shop where Dough Boy (aka Troy Elliot) applied the silver pearl paint over a gray basecoat. At the same time any parts that needed to be polished or plated went to Dave "Thurstin" Howell at Howell Racing.

The engine installed is based on a stock Harley-Davidson V-twin, with the addition of Wiseco 10.5 to 1 pistons, a Crane cam, and ported

Left Up front it's another 18 in. Avon tire and Perewitz/Sullivan wheel. Perewitz/Sullivan also provided the new fork assembly with the ultrasmooth lower legs.

Right Left side of the engine shows off the open primary (part of every proper hardtail), the solenoids for the nitrous, and the hand-built pod for the ignition and starter switch.

Harley heads. Two Edelbrock QuickSilver carburetors hang out into the air stream on the right side, and are fed gas from the stretched tank and nitrous oxide from the small tank bolted to the downtube.

A belt primary drive, contained in an open-billet housing, transfers the engine's power to a 5-speed transmission filled with Andrews gears. Another belt runs from the transmission to the rear wheel, this one a stock drive belt connected to a 70-tooth billet rear sprocket. The 70-tooth sprocket and both billet wheels come from the partnership of Dave Perewitz and Bobby Sullivan.

Front and rear rims measure 18 in. in diameter and both mount Avon tires, a130/70x18 upfront and a 180/55x18 in the rear. A single front rotor, designed to match the wheels, mounts to the left side, coupled to a 4-piston caliper from Performance Machine. At the back there's another matching rotor and one more 4-piston caliper.

A bare bones bike with an attitude, Terry's hardtail goes to show that sometimes when you delete the rear suspension, elaborate paint job, and expensive billet parts, you end up with more — more of what might be called the essential V-twin motorcycle.

Second Generation Bar Hoppers from Bob McKay

Model: Hardtail

Bob McKay from Shallow Lake, Ontario, considers himself both a franchised Harley-Davidson dealer and a custom bike builder. Among all the different types of bikes Bob has built over the years, he especially enjoyed the simple little hardtails.

The Hog Bike

The first of Bob's new/old hardtails borrows much from those old bikes he remembers so well. The frame is an Edlunds hardtail chassis from Pat Kennedy, with the look of a straight-leg frame from about 1957. This new frame is, however, designed to accept a late-model drive train.

To keep the project cheap, Bob used many left-over parts he found in the shop. The brakes, for example, were left-over when a new-bike customer replaced the stock calipers with 4-piston replacements.

The Evo engine is pretty much a stock 80 in. (203 cm) unit, made up of more recycled parts. The cases were damaged factory cases that Bob had repaired. The jugs, heads, as well as nearly everything else are more parts left from other people's upgrades. The only exceptions are the Screamin' Eagle cam and the unique Bob McKay drag pipes.

For a front fork Bob combined shortened 41 mm tubes, stock lower legs, and White Brothers springs. Arlen Ness triple trees mount the tubes to the frame in Wide Glide fashion and flat drag bars point the way. For a rear tire Bob mounted a 140x16 in. Avon tire on a stock spoked rim while in front he installed a 21 in. Metzeler on another spoked rim from Harley-Davidson.

The project's original goals ruled out the use of anything but simple sheet metal. The only deviation from that rule is the gas tank. Though it is a three-and-a-quarter gallon Sportster tank, the installation of the tachometer into the gas tank makes it a less-than-simple highlight to the rest of the bike.

Right **Bob used a Sportster tank, just like in the old days – except that this one has a very high performance pig airbrushed on either side, and a tachometer mounted right into the tank.**

BOB
HARLEY-DAVIDSON
McKAYS

If the tank is too fancy the rear fender is as simple as possible, a flat "Bob Job" supported by a welded strut. Between the tank and the fender is the small seat from Drag Specialties and below that is a McKay-special horseshoe-shaped oil tank.

A basic bike calls out for black paint – Bob understood that fact when he applied the black urethane. Bevin Finlay from Belmore, Ontario is the man responsible for the hot-rod hog on the tank, done before Bob applied the clearcoat. Once

completed, his Hog bike was not only fun to ride, but also attracted the envy of costly softail owners.

A more modern old hardtail

The red hardtail is decidedly more modern than the little hog bike.

Like the earlier bike, this one comes with no front fender and only the simplest of rear fenders.

The V-twin engine displaces a full 96 ci (1,573 cc). Not only is this one more powerful than the near-stock 80 ci (1,311 cc) motor, it's also adorned with an abundance of aluminum jewelry. The rocker boxes, camshaft cover, transmission cover, and left-side primary cover all come from the Arlen Ness catalog, carved from billet aluminum and chrome plated for maximum brilliance.

What Bob calls "new technology parts" include the brakes, which are made up of billet 4-piston calipers from RevTech, two in front and two at the back. Though the earliest hardtails ran springer forks, this red rocket uses a modern hydraulic fork assembly from Arlen Ness. The fancy fork assembly supports a 21 in. spoked rim, while at the back a new 16 in. rim mounts a new Avon tire that measures more than 7 in. across.

Bob's two bikes are both a unique mix of the old and new. Yet both are also part of the ageless less-is-more idea.

Left **This red bike uses all the fancy parts the black one didn't. The end result is a brighter, more modern, more expensive motorcycle.**

Australian Shovelhead Eats Evos

Model: Shovelhead

Most Harley-Davidson riders would agree that the newer Evolution motor is more efficient and faster than the older Shovelhead. Yet this Harman Shovelhead eats Evos as appetizers.

What looks at first like just another rigid old Harley is, in fact, a larger-than-life Shovelhead. A bike that combines John Harman engine components in a custom frame, all of it assembled by Neville Sharp of Melbourne, Australia.

The cylinders feature a full 4.325 in. (11 cm) bore and bolt to special reinforced engine cases. The oversize heads are equipped with valves the size of pistons found in 4-cylinder bikes and intake tracts designed to mount individual carburetors.

A QuickSilver 38 mm slide carburetor feeds each of the giant cylinders, while an Andrews B grind camshaft opens the intake and exhaust valves. A Crane ignition drives the coils, which are mounted up and out of the way under the gas tank. One-off upswept pipes, fabricated specially for this bike,

Left **Gas tank with Sportster profile, combined with the rigid frame and Shovelhead engine, gives the bike the look of an early chopper. Note the coils hidden up under the gas tank (each cylinder head contains two spark plugs) and the QuickSilver carburetor bolted to each cylinder head.**

Above **No two hardtails are alike. This example built by Neville Sharp of Melbourne, Australia uses a monster motor and high-grade hardware to achieve a certain raw elegance.**

provide an exit route for the spent exhaust gases.

An open belt primary, this one measuring a full 3 in. (7.6 cm) across, takes the tractor torque of this monster motor to a 4-speed transmission and Atlas clutch. A chain provides the final link between the engine and the 16 in. Dunlop rear tire. Both the belt primary and final chain drive are protected from debris and the rider's pants cuff by fabricated aluminum guards.

A 19 in. Dunlop mated to a dresser front fork assembly holds up the other end of this no-frills hauler. Both front and rear wheels mate aluminum rims with stainless spokes

to create an assembly that's both good looking as well as strong. The same regard for quality is evident in the choice of brakes. In front, a pair of 4-piston calipers from Performance Machine squeeze large-diameter floating front brake rotors, while at the rear another PM 4-piston caliper is paired to a smaller stainless steel rotor.

Neville fabricated the oil tank to include a box for the battery. The gas tank also received plenty of the customizer's attention. What seems

Left **The front end of this hardtail is simple and effective. Wide Glide fork assembly is borrowed from a Harley Dresser. Each lower leg mounts a 4-piston caliper mated to a large diameter floating rotor. 19 in. (48.2 cm) wheel assembly is made up of an aluminum rim and stainless spokes.**

to be a stock Sportster tank is actually an aftermarket Sportster tank that Neville converted from dual gas fillers to a single flush-mount cap. The Harman motor uses lots of external oil lines, all of them made from braided stainless hose with anodized aluminum fittings. The brakes are plumbed from master cylinder to caliper with similar high-grade braided components. The paint job by Tombstone covers nearly everything, including the fenders, frame, and engine drive pulley.

Hardtail With a Boost

Model: Hardtail

Not all hardtails look the same or follow traditional lines. At least this one certainly is not just another run-of-the-mill hardtail.

With narrow glide trees and 39 mm forks, this bike looks like a thin line from the rear – except for the tank where it becomes a tad wider. The fattest thing on the whole bike might be the 180x18 in. Metzeler rear tire, mounted to an Akront rim laced to a Harley-Davidson hub with Buchanan spokes. At the front is a 19 in. Metzeler tire (not a 21) mounted to another high-quality rim, spoke, and hub combination.

The front wheel is located by the 39 mm fork legs, which use tubes that are actually one inch longer than stock. Each lower leg carries a 4-piston Performance Machine caliper, and each caliper squeezes a slotted polished rotor. The back uses four more 4-piston calipers, all squeezing the same polished rotor.

Though the wheels and brakes might be top quality, it's between the wheels that this bike gets really

Right **The unusual silhouette is created in part by the unique gas tank and front fender, combined with the bike's overall length.**

interesting. A set of Delkron cases, filled with 4.6 in. (11.7 cm) of S&S flywheel assembly, was topped off by aluminum cylinders with a 3.5 in. (8.9 cm) bore from Harley-Davidson and heads from STD. The STD heads typically come in raw form, so some porting work had to be done before installing new seats, Manley valves, and 200 pound S&S valve springs.

What makes the stroker motor in this hardtail interesting is the

Aerocharger turbocharger, and the attention to detail that was used in assembling the engine.

The boost level was then set at 13 psi (90 kpa). That pressure is delivered to and through the Mikuni carburetor and eventually into the combustion chamber each time the recommended Aerocharger camshaft lifts an intake valve. In spite of the pressurized intake tract, the engine runs 9 to 1 static compression and burns pump premium gas. Detonation is not a problem, in part because the bike uses a Dyna ignition and two plugs per cylinder.

The cases and cylinders were sent to Sumax for powder coating. Rather than use black or a color to match the bike, the crew at Sumax applied a gray powder doctored up with silver pearl flakes from House of Kolor. The color is subtle and has a flip-flop effect created by the pearl flakes. Anything that didn't get powder coated has been painted to match the rest of the bike.

Inside the primary housing is a Primo belt which takes the power to a 5-speed transmission equipped with Andrews gears. Exiting the 5-speed transmission is a standard final drive belt connected to the 70 tooth billet pulley.

Left **Externally the engine is extremely sanitary, which makes the turbo installation seem more like an integral part and less like a bolt-on accessory.**

Above **19 in. front rim is laced to the Harley-Davidson hub with twisted Buchanan spokes. Fabricated fender covers the Metzeler tire.**

Fat Bob tanks would hardly fit the long and skinny theme, so three tanks were cut up to create one long enough to fit the stretched Tripoli frame. The rear fender is a fiberglass fender supported by simple steel struts.

Mark Sporka from Menomonie Falls, Wisconsin, molded all the seams on the frame and sheet metal, and applied the black paint, graphics, and clearcoat. The color is actually a black pearl and changes with the angle and type of lighting — and of course the seat came from Danny Gray, seat-maker to the stars.

A Showcase Hardtail

Model: Hardtail

The concept started when Rob and his partner Gary Strom decided it might be fun to build a "shop bike."

The "shop" in question is called Kokesh MC, a small motorcycle shop located on Highway 65 just north of Minneapolis, Minnesota. At Kokesh they have very little staff turnover, most of the crew are both diehard motorcycle fanatics and long-term employees.

Kokesh is what you might call a full-service shop. Not only do they sell parts for new and old Harley-Davidsons, they service those same bikes, restore old Knuckle- and Panheads, and build the occasional custom machine. Engine work is usually the domain of Lee Wickstrom and it was Lee who assembled the 80 ci (1,311 cc) V-twin starting with S&S engine cases and a flywheel assembly from Harley-Davidson.

Modifications include the special Lee Wickstrom cylinder heads. More than just a porting job, Lee welded up the stock ports before beginning the reshaping with the Dremel tool.

Left **The devil is in the details. Laser was used to cut the H-D logo into the metal bezel for this old Chevrolet taillight.**

Above **In terms of styling, this hardtail falls somewhere between traditional and new-wave. Red with yellow flames makes for a very intense visual package.**

Working in concert with the high-flow heads is a Viper cam from Mid-USA with 0.560 in. (1.42 cm) of lift and duration of 248 and 252 degrees for the intake and exhaust. Feeding the oversize intake tract is an oversize carburetor, the S&S Super G, normally seen on larger engines. The spark and ignition curve are provided by a Crane HI-4 ignition.

Behind the high-performance V-twin sits a high-performance 5-speed transmission. Starting with a Harley-Davidson case, close-ratio gears from Andrews were added. Engine and transmission are connected by a standard primary chain.

An Atlas wide-drive chassis with 3 in. (7.6 cm) of stretch and a 38-degree fork angle was used. These

Right **Jery Scherer, sometimes known as the Old Guy, did all the paint and prep work; including the molded frame, application of the red urethane, and even the yellow flames.**

wide-drive frames are designed to accept a fat rear tire, up to 7 in. wide. It was possible to install a 180x18 in. Metzeler tire on an RC Components billet aluminum rim and still have room for belt drive. In front, another Metzeler tire, this one a 120x18 in., was installed on another matching RC rim.

Because it's such a light bike, a single front brake was deemed more than adequate. Bolted to the left lower leg is the Performance Machine 4-piston, differential-bore caliper. For the rear wheel another Performance Machine caliper, this time a conventional 4-piston design, squeezes another stainless-steel rotor.

Both the front and rear fenders started out as aftermarket steel fenders, modified and massaged into a more pleasing and unique shape. The rear fender, in particular, was strengthened so there would be no need for conventional fender struts. At the back of the fender is a nifty taillight that started life on an old Chevrolet before being adapted to fit the end of a motorcycle fender. Just ahead of the fender is another unique piece, the wrap around oil tank that comes back into a point on the left side to provide a place to mount the ignition switch.

An aftermarket gas tank was chosen, one with a pleasing shape that seemed to fit the frame and match the lines of the two fenders. Local upholstery wizard Mark Milbrant stitched up a special seat to wrap down along the frame rails on either side. This was done to disguise the offset in the left side frame rail, which is necessary to make room for the wide rear tire.

Once the bike came apart, another local expert took over. Jerry Scherer applied the House of Kolor kosmos red urethane paint to the frame, fenders, and most of the engine. Flames done with special one-off yellow paint mixed up by Jon Kosmoski from House of Kolor were then added.

To wrap up, the unusual White Brothers Exhaust pipe, Headwinds headlight, and Krome Werks bars were all bolted in place.

The flamed hardtail is successdful as a showcase for Kokesh, and not just because it's a very clean little bar hopper. The bike works because it's just a little different from all the other hardtails out there – much the way Kokesh itself is just a little different from all the other motorcycle shops.

S&S
SUPER

HARLEY
DAVIDSON

Not Quite a Hardtail

It can be said that 1981 was a significant year in American history. Not because a war began or ended that year, or because of some enormous political scandal. The year is significant because on June 16, 1981 a group of Harley-Davidson executives signed the papers to buy the company back from American machine and foundry – making Harley-Davidson an independent company once again. Though it's hard to believe today, the success of the newly independent venture was anything but assured. AMF bought the motor company in 1969 and did much to increase production of Harley-Davidson motorcycles. Some would say, however, that increased production came at the expense of quality.

Custom Softail

Model: Softail

In 1971 Harley-Davidson introduced the first Super Glide, which later evolved into the Low Rider and eventually the Wide Glide.

Despite the basic good looks of the Super Glides and Low Riders, they relied on the Shovelhead engine, 4-speed transmission, and chain drive to the rear wheel. By the early 1980s these were dated machines (the Shovelhead first appeared in 1966) with a questionable reputation for quality.

Survival for Harley-Davidson meant the introduction of new models and updated drive trains. In 1982 Harley-Davidson introduced a new line of bikes: the FXR models with rubber-mounted engines. The next big improvement came in 1984 with the unveiling of the Evolution

engine. But there was another introduction in 1984 that played a bigger role in Harley's eventual success than any other.

Most industry insiders agree that the introduction of the Softail model in 1984 was the best marketing move ever made by Harley-Davidson. Based on a rear suspension design purchased from an individual customizer, the new chassis hid the rear shocks and springs under the frame. By using a triangulated swing arm, the new Softail had the look of the earlier Hardtail frame without the harsh ride.

Before the introduction of the Softail, Harley-Davidson had the sound that everyone wanted, afterward they had the sound and the look that defines an American motorcycle. Though the Softail chassis would eventually serve as the foundation for at least four families of machines, the first Softails made for very popular factory customs.

Some call it the bike that saved Milwaukee. More than that, however, these factory customs seemed to beg for further modification by owners. When they introduced the Softail, Harley-Davidson assured their own survival, and also the survival of hundreds of small customizing and aftermarket shops.

Things haven't changed all that much in the ensuing years. Softails are still the most popular bikes built by Harley-Davidson, and they still beg for further refinement by the owners.

The bikes seen here represent an overview of the multitude of Softails customized, painted, and rebuilt in garages all over the world. Some of the owners reach backward with early sheet metal and springer forks to create a new bike that looks genuinely old, while other owners install the latest billet aluminum wheels and accessories, and apply the brightest neon colors imaginable.

Left **The Fat Bob tanks on this custom Softail were streched to match the frame.**

Above **At the front of this Softail creation by Jon Dasheur is a factory style disk brake and a new spoked wheel with chrome rim and 16 in. Metzeler tire.**

A Modern Seamless Softail

Model: Softail

This orange Softail might be called the evolutionary end of a series. The smoothness of the machine starts dead center with the special one-piece Fat Bob tanks and integral dash.

Bob at Carefree Highway Truckin' in Tulsa, Oklahoma is responsible for all the nice metal and molding work. Bob started with separate 5 gallon Fat Bob tanks and a dash from Pro One. By the time he was done, the two tanks and single dash were magically merged into one seamless piece.

The transformation started with a new extended tail for each tank. Because the two tanks were to be made one, Bob had to design a new "drop on" mounting system in place of the standard side mounts used on late model Fat Bob tanks. After welding the two tanks into one unit,

Bob welded on the metal dash from Pro One.

He then created the rear fender by first widening a Fat Boy rear fender, and then welding it to a pair of Pro One fender struts. Before he was finished, Bob added a flush-mount LED tail, brake light, and a nifty slide-in-from-behind license plate mounting system. Unlike the rear fender, the Fat Boy front fender was left in an "as stamped" condition and prepped for paint.

Everything on the bike was molded, including all fabrication work, as well as the welds on the Pro One frame. The orange paint is actually a tangelo pearl hue from the House of Kolor sprayed over a white base. Once Bob finished with the paint, Cole Stevens added airbrush graphics before turning the parts over to The Wizard for final pinstriping.

The V-twin in this orange crush measures 80 ci (1,311 cc) and was designed to be a dependable, fun, street motor.

In place of stock components, Donny Meador at Kinetic Playground in Tulsa used a Head Quarters camshaft and pushrods, a Super E carburetor from S&S, a Dyna S ignition, and pipes from Vance & Hines. The motor is so bright it's hard to look at on a sunny day. The cases are polished while the cylinders are de-finned, and then painted orange to match the bike. Chrome-plated rocker boxes top it all off, complimented by a plated primary cover, billet derby and inspection covers, and an Arlen Ness cam cover.

Even the transmission case was polished before being filled with Andrews gears and a roller bearing trap door. A BDL belt-drive primary

Left **Shaun Christian's orange Softail gets much of its sleek appearance from the stretched Pro One frame and the 38 degree fork angle.**

connects engine and transmission, while a stock belt is used between the transmission and rear wheel.

The final-drive belt mates to a RC Components 70 tooth rear sprocket, which in turn bolts to a RC 18x5.5 in. billet-wheel equipped with an Avon 180 series tire. A matching 18 in. wheel, this one equipped with a 3.5 in. rim, mounts between the 39 mm wide glide fork legs. Polished PM 4-piston calipers, one on each end, squeeze ventilated rotors to slow everything down.

When all the outside craftsmen were finished, Shaun and crew assembled the engine and transmission, fenders, wheels, calipers, and rotors into a complete motorcycle. As part of the final assembly, all the wiring was hidden inside the frame, and the ignition switch moved to a small housing just behind the rear cylinder. Final hardware choices include a Headwinds headlight, billet forward controls from PM, and grips from Arlen Ness. The neatly fitting solo seat is the handwork of Southeast Auto Trim in Tulsa.

The end result of all the careful planning, fabrication, and assembly is a very professional and finished motorcycle. What you might call a seamless Softail.

Right **The Wizard seen on the dash is the result of airbrush work from the talented Mr. Stevens.**

Left **The ignition switch on this seamless beauty has been moved to the pod below the seat, and all the wiring routed inside the frame. Engine cases, cylinder, and heads have all been polished. Cylinders and heads were then painted orange, between the fins, to match the rest of the bike.**

New Parts Make an Old Motorcycle

Model: Softail

The idea here was to build a "springer," but not the typical chopper-style of springer with a long fork and 21 in. (53 cm) front wheel.

Of course, the first big problem was finding a front fork, because at that time Harley didn't make a springer designed to run a 16 in. (40.6 cm) wheel. So the obvious choice was a 2 in. (5 cm)-under fork from Sundance and an early style front fender from V-Twin.

Mating the V-Twin fender to the Sundance fork proved a difficult task for at least two reasons. First, the fender had to be narrowed to make it fit between the legs of the fork. Second, a linkage had to be designed that would keep the fender the same distance from the tire as the tire went up and down over bumps.

Paul Chergosky from Anoka, Minnesota is the man responsible for the modified fork. He's also the man who designed and installed the support assembly up inside the Softail rear fender and figured out how to mount it to the frame with four bolts hidden under the seat. The whole idea of course was to make this look like a more convincing hardtail from 1936. The stubby fork and strut-less rear fender bolt to a Paughco Softail-style frame. Because the goal was a retro bike, the frame without any

Left **The engine in Jon's machine is an 80 ci (1,311 cc) Evo built with a combination of aftermarket and Harley-Davidson parts. Early style oil filter, horn, and exhaust work in harmony with the styling cues used throughout the bike.**

additional rake or stretch was ordered. Up front, the light bar and brackets that mount the headlight and spotlights were fabricated. In back, an early-style 5-bar luggage rack was purchased, and then narrowed to hold only four bars and better fit the proportions of the bike. In order to accommodate an occasional passenger, a pillion pad from Corbin that bolts to the same four holes used to mount the luggage rack was used.

Tracy at TJ Design in Shakopee, Minnesota molded the frame and sheet metal, and then painted the bike and frame in vibrant blue. Both the front and rear fenders were then edged in silver and gold leaf. The tanks received the same treatment, a combination of silver leaf in the

***Above* The large diameter headlight and twin spotlights all mount to a fabricated light bar. Bullet shaped clearance lights are used as turn signals.**

shape of an eagle's claw, with a diamond shaped gold leaf inset, pinstriped and lettered by hand. Multiple clearcoats bury the ultra thin strips of metal and pinstriping so the paint surface is both seamless and ultraglossy.

The power for this retro springer comes from a 80 ci (1,311 cc) Evo style engine based on STD cases combined with Harley-Davidson cylinders and heads. The relatively mild V-twin uses a Keihin CV-style carburetor equipped with a Harley-Davidson air cleaner and two-in-one exhaust complete with a

fishtail tip. The cylinders are painted blue to match the bike while the heads are painted silver. Primary, cam, and derby covers are all made-in-Milwaukee items. The derby and inspection covers carry the Harley logo in gold in order to match the air cleaner, fenders, and tank.

Left **To create a true Hardtail impression, Jon Dasheur used a rear fender with no external struts. Beehive taillight, rear support stand, and an early style luggage rack all work to create the look of a 1936 Harley VL.**

American Thunder in Shakopee, Minnesota helped with the final assembly of the bike. Neal and the crew installed the engine and stock 5-speed transmission, and connected the two with a BDL primary belt. Another belt, this one from Harley-Davidson, carries the power from the transmission to the 16 in. (40.6 cm) rear wheel. Forward controls for the 5-speed tranny and the Harley-Davidson rear disk brake are from Jay Brake.

In addition to the highway pegs, floor boards were put up front. At back, a beehive taillight was chosen that flanked on either side by simple early-style marker lights, used in this case as blinkers. Below the fender lip hangs the old-style stand; like many of the parts on this bike, the stand had to be modified to fit, and then sent out to Brown's for chrome plating. Final assembly details include the chrome wrap used on all the cables, the invisible wiring, and the early-style horn and oil filter.

More than money, this project required time: time to find the right parts, the right artists, and the right mechanics who could transform a certain new/old motorcycle from fantasy to reality.

A Two-Wheeled Canvas

Model: Softail

The goal was a bike that would be one integral unit, one whole piece of mechanical art. Each part of the puzzle needed to blend with the others instead of standing alone.

The sheet metal that required so much hard work bolts to the remains of a 1995 Harley-Davidson Softail chassis. The modified frame is nearly 3 in. (7.6 cm) longer than a stocker, and mounts the fork at a longish 38 degree angle.

The 41 mm wide glide fork assembly from the original bike is now mated to Dresser lower legs with caliper mounting lugs on either side. The 4-piston calipers are from PM and each one carries the special milled pattern that is used throughout the bike. The trick one-off billet aluminum triple trees, carved on CNC equipment, feature a stepped design and internal hydraulic circuits so the brake lines actually thread into the lower triple tree instead of a conventional "T". Between the two fork legs is a 21 in.

Right **It's hard to tell that this was once a FXSTC (Softail Custom). The frame has been stretched, the rake has been increased, and personalized sheet metal designs and elaborate paint work were applied.**

billet wheel from Arlen Ness, rotating on a flush-mount Donnie Smith axle.

Milwaukee Iron did the rough sheet metal fabrication to exact specifications. The tanks fit very precisely to the neck area, and the dash fits with such precision that the two tanks merge and become one. The raw fender with its internal support was crafted by Randy from Milwaukee Iron. The design includes a seat that is Frenched into the fender, and repeats the graphic design seen in the paint. The seat pan and

ZJ6507

Above **An elaborate paint job required that each spear and arch be masked off separately. Then Andy Anderson would apply the basecoat followed by multiple coats of a special-mix candy color. After, drying spear could be masked over and Andy would start on another area.**

Left **Note how the fabricated rear fender seems an extension of the gas tank – all of it tied together by the flow of the sheet metal, and complex paint job.**

detailed sketches were sent to Danny Gray, who earned undying respect for crafting the perfect seat. Like all the panels on this bike, the side covers blend right into the rear fender, though they are separate pieces.

The swingarm is another piece of fine art. Crafted from the original, the triangular design uses covers, painted to match the bike, to hide the axle nuts, with small stainless vents at the front of the design. In order to run the wide 160x17 in. tire, a relatively narrow billet pulley and drive belt designed for a Sportster were used.

Painted in candy magenta and hot pink, the engine for the artistic two-wheeler measures 89 ci (1,458 cc). External refinements include polished factory cases, and special milled patterns that run diagonally across each cylinder, the work of John Bryant in Cleveland, Ohio. Derby, inspection, and transmission covers all come from the Florida shop of Clyde McCullough.

The extra cubes were obtained with a stroker, 4.6 in. (11.7 cm) flywheel assembly from S&S, mated to cylinders with stock internal dimensions. The Harley heads were converted to dual plug status and encouraged to flow more air with help from Red Rhea at R&B Cycles in Nashville. A pair of Quicksilver carbs mounted behind a billet air cleaner feed gas and air to the stroker motor each time the Crane cam opens one of Red's massaged intake valves. Exhaust valves dump into a pair of very unique pipes – the best excuse to buy a TIG welder.

After assembling the complete machine, minus the engine, the whole thing was sprayed with yellow base coat mixed from House of Kolor Shimrins. This was followed-up with a very complex layout with thin fine line tape. Next, all the graphic areas received a silver basecoat before application of the House of Kolor kandies could begin. Each spear and oval was created in multiple stages, blending various mixes of kandies so each one contains subtle color changes and shadings. That same fanaticism was used in the handle bars. Beyond a mild custom, Andy's fanaticism created a unique piece of two-wheeled mechanical art.

Right **Andy Anderson spent considerable time doing sketches and colored renderings of this bike before he decided on the design he really liked. The goal was a machine where each fender or exhaust pipe became a blended portion of the overall machine.**

Right Left side shows off the polished cases, polished and painted cylinders and heads, and the unique diagonal pattern milled into the cylinders. Derby and inspection covers are one-off designs created just for this bike.

It Was Supposed to be Easy

Model: Softail

The ultrawide rear tire of this bike required a new rear fender. But it was during this discussion of fenders that the project began to get out of hand.

Instead of mounting a catalog fender with the standard fender struts, Mike McAllister at M-C Specialties in Blaine, Minnesota suggested that he could create a trick fender with internal struts. The idea was readily agreed to and that might have been the end of the matter – except for one thing. Mike also recommended that a whole new front frame section with better esthetics and additional stretch be created instead of just adding to the rake. Again, this was agreed, and Mike and his merry crew went to work building a new rear fender and a complete front frame section.

Installing the new swingarm meant disassembly of the primary drive on the bike's left side. Once the primary drive and most of the sheet metal was removed, Mike was about two bolts short of having the motor out of the frame.

Pulling the motor out of the frame would open up a whole raft of creative possibilities. Up to this point the plan was to paint the new frame

Right **Whether they're 2-wheelers or 4-wheelers, all true hot rods have fat tires. This 200 series Avon mounts to a 6 in. wide rim so it's just a little wider than the same tire on a 5 in. rim.**

Left **Left side shows the stretched tanks with trim dash. Cylinders and heads have been polished and painted. Chrome primary cover and billet floorboards add more shine to this already bright machine.**

MINNESOTA
PITBUL

section black to match the existing frame, and then simply paint the new rear fender to match the sheet metal. But Mike decided to revise his original plan, and decided that a bright paint job by local craftsman Bruce Bush would be worth the cost.

This meant that Mike could fabricate handle bars from stainless-steel tubing. Like the bars, the seat is a one-off crafted by Kevin Lehan. Because the rear fender has no provision for a taillight, Mike used a side-mount license plate bracket and light assembly.

Though it was elected to leave the already modified engine alone, a new coil bracket and covers were added to the left side. The bracket also contains the ignition and start switch which took all the switches off the handle bars. The simplified wiring meant a simplified harness, one that Mike could hide inside the frame before beginning the reassembly.

As the bike came back together there were a few more snags. The 200 series tire mounted on a 6 in. Performance Machine rim did fit, but left no room for the existing brakes. The answer: new brakes from Performance Machine. With everything gleaming and new, the old exhaust system just wouldn't do, so Mike installed a new pipe and muffler combination from Vance & Hines. Most of the plated or polished parts went to either Brown's Plating

***Right* The engine in Tom's new softail is a "hot rod 80" – a motor with increased power obtained through the use of a performance carburetor, camshaft, pipes, and ignition.**

***Left* Mike and Tom used a 19 in. front tire from Avon, mounted to a PM wheel and slowed by a single PM caliper. The new front frame section includes the front downtubes, which are larger diameter than stock, for a beefier look.**

in Texas or Deter's Polishing in nearby Fridley.

Like a snowball tumbling downhill, the project that Tom and Mike first conceptualized picked up speed and momentum as it rolled. The project that was supposed to be easy to do and relatively inexpensive to complete, turned out to be neither easy nor cheap.

More Challenging Than Most

Model: Softail

When Chrome Specialties asked him to build a bike based on a number of their new products, well-known bike builder Donnie Smith didn't think the job would be too tough. Not, that is, until they specified which parts he had to use and what kind of a look they wanted the bike to have.

Not surprisingly, most of the parts on this bike come from the Chrome Specialties (often abbreviated CSI) catalog. The Jammer Softail-style frame arrived at Donnie's shop with no stretch and a modest rake angle. Donnie immediately did what he calls a "wedge rake" to increase the fork angle to about 37 degrees. The fork itself is an inverted design, said to be stronger because these assemblies mount the larger diameter part of the fork in the triple trees so that less flexing occurs during braking and cornering.

While the forks might be great, the triple trees that came with the forks left much to be desired. Hence, Donnie built his own triple trees

Right **Sputhe rocker boxes top off the polished and painted cylinders and heads. Cam cover and transmission right side cover carry a Donnie Smith design. Fat tanks and Street Sweeper air cleaner cover show off the graphic talents of Lenni Schwartz.**

from aluminum. The trees that came with the forks looked pretty chunky with big pinch bolts that stuck out. Donnie made a pair of trees with hidden bolts as well as a split in the backside, where one can't see it. The forks were also taken apart and the springs changed to lower the front end of the bike by about two inches.

At the other end of the bike Donnie and crew installed the X-Drive swingarm, one of the new products that Donnie designed for CS1. The X-Drive makes it possible to install a 200x16 in. tire in a standard Softail frame.

Key to the whole project was the use of the new, extra large, 7 gallon Fat Bob gas tanks. Rob Roehl, Donnie's sheet metal man, formed sheet metal tails for the end of each tank. With the extensions in place, the tanks wrap around the front edge of the seat and extend back to neatly meet the frame rails. The dash was stretched by extending the Jammer dash to come back all the way to the edge of the custom Keith Nybo seat.

To power the new rotund motorcycle Donnie ordered a 96 ci (1,573 cc) engine complete from S&S. Instead of buying the motor already assembled, Donnie bought it in parts, so the fins on the cylinders and heads could be polished before the cases, cylinders, and heads were painted in purple to match everything else. Don Tima, Donnie's engine man, then carefully assembled all the new parts into a complete V-twin.

The complete 5-speed transmission, primary chain, and final belt drive all came from the CSI catalog. Before installation, the transmission case received a coat of that same purple paint, a chrome top cover, and a new Donnie Smith side cover.

The trend in spoked wheels is to increase the amount of spokes, so Donnie chose 80-spoke wheels from Hallcraft, a 16x3.5 in. in front and a 16x5 in. in the back. Three floating rotors, two in front and one at the back, matched to 4-piston Motor Factory brake calipers provide premium braking power for the big, purple Packard.

Another interesting innovation is the handle bars. Unlike most bars, these are made from 1.5 in. (3.8 cm) tubing, so the bars are the same size as the mounts for the master cylinder and the CSI grips. The big bars look so clean that one wonders why nobody did this before.

This massive bike gets its look from the larger-than-life sheet metal, the fat tires used on both ends, and the passion purple House of Kolor paint applied by Brian Mahler with graphics by Lenni Schwartz.

If Donnie had doubts about the bike when he started, those doubts were quickly erased by the time the bike rolled out of the shop for the first time. Public reaction to Moby Grape has since been astounding – it draws a crowd wherever it is parked. What started out as a challenging project turned out to be a huge success.

Above Right **Until recently the inverted fork designs were seen only on competition or sport bikes. This 34 mm design from CSI fits most current Harley-Davidsons. The upside down forks give riders a stronger assembly, and a new look for the front of the bike.**

Left **Fat is where it's at. Donnie's crew stretched the tanks to wrap around the front of the seat and then stretched the dash to match. Note the large-diameter bars and the billet speedometer cover.**

A Home-Run Hit

Model: Softail

If Donnie Smith's purple bike is a bit on the heavy side, then the orange machine is at the other end of the scale.

Like a young athlete, this orange Softail is trim and taut, unable to relax, always ready to compete. And like a professional athlete, each part of the machine contributes to the overall sense of perfection. At the front, this bike rides on a slim 19 in. Avon tire mounted on a Performance Machine wheel. The narrow-glide fork is a Donnie Smith original, made up by installing 41 mm fork tubes in fabricated aluminum triple trees. Twin 6-piston calipers from Performance Machine are mounted on the Pro One lower legs on either side, with rotors from PM designed to match the wheels.

The front wheel with its skinny hot rod fender seems to reach out ahead of the bike, placed there by the 38 degree fork angle. There is no air dam between the front wheel and the frame; instead this bike carries a belly pan that gives a much more finished look to the Daytec frame.

The long, slim gas tank is a perfect fit for the rest of the bike. If you ask Donnie how he achieved such a nice shape for the tank, he gives all the credit to his metal man, "We started with an aftermarket tank, a Mustang tank," explains Donnie. "I just gave the tank to Rob and he did his magic. Part of what makes it such a nice shape is the raised section along the top, it gives the tank some character and makes it seem longer."

Behind the tank is a one-off solo seat built by Keith Nybo and behind that is the minimalist fender with internal struts, more of Rob's handiwork. While some oil tanks just sit there, this one fits snugly into the curve of the frame, the gap between the tank and frame exactly the same all along the top and the back side.

Contributing to the long lean look of this bike are the hand-fabricated exhaust pipes. The two pipes run side by side, fairly high up on the bike. Each is marred by only a small bulge. The pipes are slash-cut at the end, with the angle of the slash perfectly matching the angle of the swingarm.

An athlete needs to be able to run and run hard. With 113 ci (1,852 cc) of V-twin heart, there aren't many street machines that this bike can't outrun.

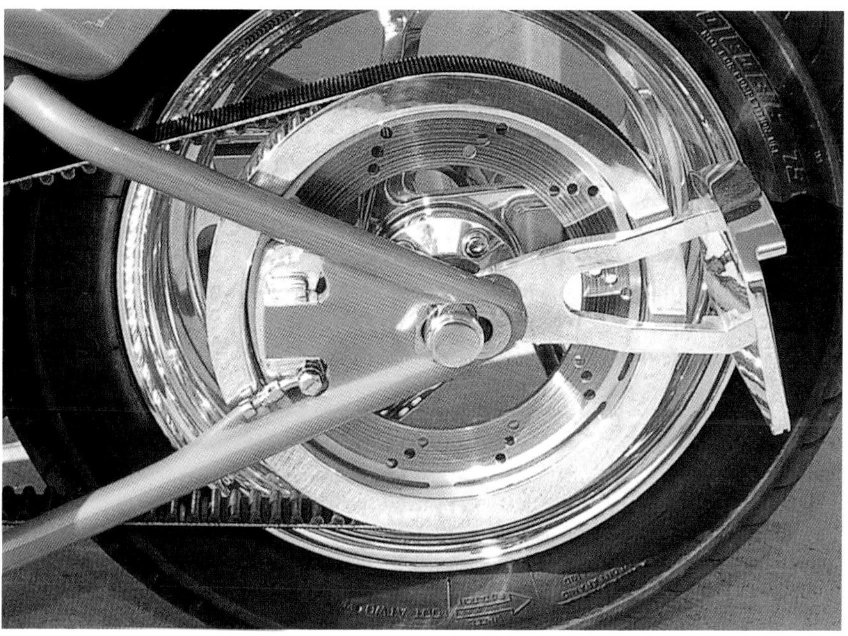

Above **If you look very closely you see the brake caliper mounted in the center of the swingarm, and the rotor mounted to the rim of the rear wheel pulley. The brake line runs inside the tubing for the rear swingarm.**

Based on the new 4 in. (10 cm) bore S&S cases and cylinders, this particular combination uses a 4.5 in. (11.3 cm) flywheel assembly to achieve the massive displacement figure. Purchased in pieces, the cylinders and heads were polished and then painted orange, like the engine cases and even the transmission.

Don Tima, engine man for Donnie Smith, carefully balanced the flywheels before proceeding with the rest of the engine assembly. Internally, this engine has all brand new S&S components, each chosen for fit and maximum mechanical harmony. Externally, the engine shines with paint, polish, or chrome, the parts chosen for simplicity and visual impact. Look closely, and you will see that even the grade 8 chrome Allen bolts have small chrome caps.

All that horsepower needs a good connection to the ground. The 200x16 Avon rear tire mounted on another

Performance Machine wheel might be called the Nike Air of motorcycle tires. On the left side of the 5-spoke wheel is one of the mechanical features that helps to put this bike in a class by itself. The very compact brake caliper sits in the apex of the swingarm where it almost disappears. If the motorcycle aftermarket gave awards for "Best Engineered New Product," this rear

Left Braided oil line leading up to the right side transmission case means this is a hydraulic, not cable-actuated, clutch. The motor on modern customs does more than power the machine – the good ones also contribute to the overall visual package. Note the polished and painted cylinders and heads, the painted engine and transmission cases, the phenomenal attention to detail.

brake would be sure to take top honors. Not only is the caliper mounting unobtrusive, the rotor is bolted to the inside of the rear brake pulley and the brake line runs inside the swingarm. The whole package, developed jointly by Donnie and Leo Di Orio, is extremely trim, compact, and well-engineered.

Donnie built the bike for James Shapiro, who chose the color after seeing an orange Panhead in the shop before construction started on his own bike. The color is actually tangelo from the House of Kolor, applied by Brain Mahler. The seamless frame is the result of Greg Smith's careful molding, and the unusual tribal-like flames are by Lenni Schwartz.

Perfection is certainly the most difficult, and even impossible, thing to achieve. For any kind of athlete it only comes after endless training. But, for a certain tangelo motorcycle, the person doing the training is the builder, who after over 20 long years of building custom motorcycles, must feel as though he has just hit another great home run over the fence and out onto the street.

Dare To Be Different

Model: Softail

"Full custom" for Dave Perewitz means a longer bike with the front wheel pushed out ahead of the frame. To meet these parameters, Dave's crew cut off the front of the frame and built a new tubular extension.

The net result is a frame 3 in. (7.6 cm) longer than stock with a fork angle of 36 degrees.What sets this bike apart from other Dave Perewitz bikes are the long fenders. These were a departure for Dave, who normally runs rather abbreviated fenders on both the front and rear. Underneath the long fenders are two 18 in. Avon tires mounted on Perewitz/Sullivan billet wheels. The sidewalls read 130/80x18 in front and 180/55x18 in back. In order to mount the wide 18 in. tire the boys at Cycle Fab re-engineered the stock swingarm to make room for both the fat-attack tire and the factory belt drive.

Right **The too blue Softail uses no graphics, just blue urethane for the stretched tanks, fenders, air cleaner, and even the rear fender struts. A big fan of the ultrasanitary look, Perewitz bikes use no gauges on the bars and just a simple smooth non-dash between the tanks. Note the air cleaner cover designed to mimic the shape of the tank, as well as the Perewitz/Sullivan fork assembly and billet wheels.**

The long stretched gas tanks are more typical of a Dave Perewitz custom. Jed, metal man at Cycle Fab, started with 5 gallon Fat Bob tanks and added tails that stretch the tanks to fit the longer frame and wrap around the front of the Danny Gray seat. Between the tanks is the typical understated Perewitz dash with no speedometer, no tach, no warning lights, and no ignition switch.

The missing ignition switch can be found on the left side, between the

Right **Sleek fender struts mount the fender low over the rear tire. GMA caliper is mounted directly below the axle, instead of in the apex of the swingarm. The swingarm itself had to be modified so David's crew could mount the 180x18 in. rear tire**

coils in the Perewitz billet coil bracket. By eliminating the turn signals David was able to eliminate any switches on the Arlen Ness handle bars.

When the time came to do something with the engine it didn't make much sense to install a mild 80 ci (1,311 cc) engine in the stretched frame with the smart sheet metal. After breaking the engine down to the bare cases, all the external pieces went to Rhode Island Tech for polishing. Next, the cylinders and heads were carefully masked off so the areas between the fins could be painted blue to match the rest of the bike.

Al Wenkus from Waltham, Massachusetts, gathered up all the polished and painted pieces and assembled them into a running whole. Al used a 4.6 in. (11.7 cm) stroker flywheel assembly coupled with 3.5-pistons, both from S&S, to create an 89 ci (1,458 cc) V-twin. On top of the cylinders are the Harley-Davidson heads with new valves and a porting job by Jim Thompson.

A Crane camshaft opens the intake and exhaust valves, allowing the stroker to inhale through a Mikuni carburetor and exhale into a set of Bub exhaust pipes. Perewitz billet rocker boxes top off the heads, while Arlen Ness cam and primary covers add more sparkle to either side of the V-twin.

Fast motorcycles need effective brakes, and Dave chose a single GMA 4-piston brake caliper at the front, squeezing a polished rotor designed to match the wheels. When it came

time to choose a fork, Dave picked one of his own super-smooth Wide-Glide assemblies. At the back the true-blue bike uses Progressive shocks designed to lower the rear by about 1 inch. The rear brakes mimic those on the front with another GMA caliper and another rotor designed to match the wheels. On the left side is another shiny piece of aluminum intended to match the design of the wheels, the 70-tooth belt pulley.

Before final assembly, Russ and Don at Cycle Fab molded the frame and all the sheet metal components to eliminate any seams and prepped the parts for paint. The true-blue paint is a pearl hue from House of Kolor, applied by Russ and David in the Cycle Fab paint booth. In keeping with the bike's dare-to-be-different theme, David chose to delete the standard graphics package and leave the bike in straight blue.

The end result is a typically sanitary Perewitz custom with a twist. A true-blue beauty with new-wave fenders and absolutely no graphics.

A Shovelheaded Softail

Model: Softail

In a very short space of time, the venerable Shovelhead engine has developed from current powerplant to nearly antique status.

Evolution engines, introduced in 1984, have become so dominant that no one even thinks about building a custom bike with a Shovelhead engine. Of course there are exceptions to every rule. Jesse Keen from Harrisburg, Pennsylvania, and his longtime friend and bike builder Ed Kerr, put together a plan to transform an old Shovelhead into something longer, brighter, and much more modern – yet still powered by the Shovelhead engine. The duo elected to stay with the old FX frame from The Motor Company. Ed thought that with a little imagination and a lot of fabrication, he could transform the old frame into a more modern foundation for a new bike.

The fabrication Ed had in mind went beyond the standard stretch and rake treatment. He borrowed the suspension geometry from a standard Softail, but he still had to determine where on the frame to locate the mount for the shocks. For a swingarm Ed elected to keep the stock piece, with a new fabricated

Right **Though it has been molded and extended, the frame underneath that gorgeous sheet metal is pure Harley-Davidson. The long frame, Arlen Ness fenders, and stretched tanks give the bike a very modern flavor.**

Right **The Arlen Ness front fender wraps around a 21 in. spoked rim. Twin Performance Machine calipers squeeze ventilated rotors.**

mount for the shocks. The actual fabrication and welding is the work of Randy Wolfe from Mechanicsburg, Pennsylvania. Randy, who spends most of his time fabricating race car frames, also created a new front frame section which stretches the bike five inches and helps to give it those nice lines.

Hanging on the long, stretched frame is a pair of long, stretched gas tanks. Ed added extra metal at the back of the tanks, mounted them low, and gave the bottom of the tanks a concave shape. For fenders he used Tail Draggers from the Arlen Ness catalog, a thin one in front and a standard 8 in. (20.3 cm) wide model in the rear. Rather than mount the taillight on the fender, Ed chose to build a small bracket, supported by tubular aluminum, to hold both the taillight and the license plate bracket. As part of the smooth and modern treatment, Ed and Jesse decided that the battery had to move from its stock external location to the center of the wraparound oil tank.

The Wide Glide forks are supported by polished Billet Concept triple trees and the lower legs are brand new units from Custom Chrome. The twin 4-piston calipers used at the front carry the familiar PM logo, as does the matching caliper used in the back. Spoked wheels, measuring 21 in. (53.3 cm) in front and 16 in. (40.6 cm) the rear, help the bike retain a classic flavor.

Mike Magaro from Harrisburg did a complete overhaul on the Shovelhead. The rebuild included the installation of a new stroker flywheel assembly from S&S, and an Andrews 485 B-grind cam. In order to ensure that those enlarged ports get enough air and fuel, Mike used a new S&S Shorty carburetor hidden under a billet air cleaner from Arlen Ness.

Right **The billet air cleaner, chrome-plated rocker boxes, polished cylinders and heads, all make the old Shovelhead sparkle. The early style engine helps give this bike a classic flavor.**

Externally, the engine and 4-speed transmission are as bright as Librandis Plating in Middletown, Pennsylvania, could make them. The cylinders are minus the bottom fins and polished to a high luster. The heads suffer from an overdose of tripoli polishing compound, and the rocker boxes are chrome-plated. Both the engine and transmission cases are fully polished and all the covers, brackets, and levers are either polished or plated.

Before the final assembly, Dave Perewitz and his brother Donnie molded the frame, smoothed the sheet metal seams, and then applied the Porsche cobalt blue from the House of Kolor. Roy Mason and Nancy Brooks did the graphics, before the Perewitz brothers applied the final clearcoats.

Final assembly took place in Ed's small shop just in time to ship it off for its first trip to Sturgis.

A Rowdy Custom

Model: Softail

The uniqueness of Jeff Beebe's black ride goes beyond the dimensions and starts at the front fork – the speedometer is attached to the left lower leg.

The rear chain sprocket on the left side was used for both sprocket and brake rotor. The Performance Machine brake caliper rides in a caliper bracket that Jeff designed, carved from a billet of aluminum by his friends at AARC Engineering. The result is a rear wheel free of visual distractions on the right side. While Jeff was making the sprocket do two jobs, he decided to make the caliper bracket do three by designing it to function as an axle spacer and part of the license plate bracket. The wheel itself is carved from aluminum by RC Components and measures 16 in. (40.6 cm) in diameter and 6 in. (15.2 cm) across, wide enough for a 200 series Avon tire, which was then the widest motorcycle tire manufactured. If the rear fender looks a bit unusual, it could be because it was designed originally for a boat trailer. The unusual fender was mounted close to the tire in a unique fashion. Instead of bolting the fender to the frame with massive fender struts, it was attached to the swingarm so that it moves up and down with the tire.

Normally the rear of the seat is supported by the fender, but the moving fender made that an unworkable solution. The solution was the custom solo seat seen here, with a small passenger pillion. The pillion is part of an oversize metal plate. When you want to carry a passenger, slide the pillion plate into a small opening behind the seat where it is supported by slots anchored to the frame.

Just ahead of the seat is the very long gas tank, stretched by the metal smiths at AARC to match the frame. The front fender is a modified Harley-Davidson item designed for a 21 in. (53 cm) front wheel. The wheel is supported by a 41 mm fork assembly and slowed by a pair of Performance Machine brake calipers squeezing 10 in. (25.4 cm) rotors.

A rowdy bike needs a rowdy engine, so a 96 ci (1, 573 cc) stump puller from S&S with a 3.6 in. (9.1 cm) bore and a 4.6 in. (11.7 cm) stroke was chosen.

The S&S heads were ported to flow more air and then installed an S&S

Above **21 in. front wheel and 38 degree rake give Jeff's bike a sense of motion, like it's already moving or at least ready to lunge ahead. Note the speedo on the fork's lower leg and the headlight housing with the long pointed shape.**

camshaft with 0.562 in. (1.43 cm) of lift and 269 degrees of duration. The carburetor is the larger, Model G, from S&S, while the exhaust pipes are Big Guns from Samson.

Behind the torque monster motor is a 5-speed transmission with a polished case outside and James gears inside. Connecting the engine and transmission is a 3 in. (9.6 cm) BDL primary belt used in place of the stock chain, contained in an open housing that Jeff designed to work with the design of the wheels.

The black paint is the work of Ted Cordts at Bootleg Paint in Chino, California. Steve Vanderman at Bootleg painted the graphics based on a sketch of a tribal design.

In all the parking lots of all bike events, one will not come by a custom bike quite as long, or for that matter, quite as rowdy as this extra-long Softail with its big motor and tribal look.

S&S

Rubber Rides

When Harley-Davidson created the first FXR model late in 1981, they combined the rubber isolating system, already used in the Dresser line, with the looks of the Super Glide. The bikes were at first called Super Glide 11 but soon evolved into their own line.

A few diehard traditionalists thought the FXR models too modern. Riders who tried out the FXR, however, soon discovered that the rubber mounting system left the best parts of the Harley experience intact. Though one of these bikes might shake a little at idle, everything smoothes out as soon as you drop it in gear and let out the clutch.

Harley-Davidson rethought the rubber-mounted concept and introduced the Dyna line, which uses a simplified rubber mounting system that works just as well as the FXR mounting system.

What these bikes have in common is the rubber mounting system for the engine. Apart from that, each bike uses a different combination of frame, wheel design, and paint job to achieve an original look, all of its own.

A Liner From the Shadley Brothers

Model: Dyna

Sportsters, FXR's, and a wide variety of customs – Mark Shadley has built them all.

What Mark really loves, however, is a bike that combines the good looks of the best customs with the power of a true hot rod. The new bikes from Arlen Ness, what Arlen calls his Luxury Liners, caught Mark's eye and he decided to have one. Mark didn't want to build just any old motorcycle. Instead of bolting in an engine with huge cubic inches, he decided to make a smaller engine perform like a big one – with the addition of a turbocharger kit from Aerocharger.

The start of the turbo adaptation actually began inside the motor. Stock Harley-Davidson flywheels in new, polished STD cases were installed. On the other end of the connecting rods are 3.5 in. Wiseco pistons with extra-thick crowns to better withstand the pressure and heat of turbocharging. The Harley heads received Black Diamond valves, and were operated by the Aerocharger camshaft.

The turbo heat shield, the chrome exhaust pipe, and most of the brackets used to mount the turbo and intercooler, were all fabricated in the Shadley Brothers shop. The rest of the engine is equally detailed: with hexed, painted, and polished cylinders, polished and painted heads, camshaft, and primary covers from Arlen Ness, and rocker box covers from Dave Perewitz. Bolted directly to the back of the engine is the polished case for the 5-speed transmission, equipped with chrome-plated top and side covers. A stock belt drive takes the power from the 5-speed transmission to the Perewitz/Sullivan billet aluminum rear wheel.

Instead of opting for a superwide rear tire, Mark used a modest 140x18 in. Avon tire at the back and 130x18 in front, mounted on another Perewitz billet wheel. Supporting the front wheel are the painted lower legs, which slide up and down on 39 mm tubes mounted in Arlen Ness billet triple trees. On the left side a 4-piston Arlen Ness caliper was installed, coupled to a

Above **The air plenum for the turbo system gave Mark a good place to put the Shadley Brothers logo. Polished fins and chrome-plated billet covers help create an engine every bit as bright as the rest of the bike.**

stainless-steel rotor cut in the same pattern as the billet wheels.

The rest of the bike is mostly Luxury Liner. Fenders from Jesse James, a stretched Arlen Ness gas tank, and a seat from Danny Gray were all mounted with Shadley Brothers brackets. Most of the switches are located on the bars, though the wiring is routed inside the Arlen Ness handlebars. The turbo installation requires a certain amount of extra hardware, like the electric fuel pump, which was hidden under the seat with the ignition coils and the battery.

A wild bike needs a wild paint job, and this one started with the application of a purple base color at the Cycle Fab shop. But what really sets this bike apart are the graphics that were then done by the talented Nancy Brooks.

Danny Builds a Dyna

Model: Dyna Glide

When Danny Gray, manufacturer of custom seats for Harley-Davidsons, decided it was time for a new ride, he called on good friend and well-known custom bike builder, Dave Perewitz.

Though some people might have started with a used bike or an aftermarket frame, Danny asked Dave Perewitz to go out and order a brand new Dyna Glide from the local dealer. Dave's Cycle Fab crew began the project by taking things off the motorcycle until they were left with a bare frame. In order to get the length called for in David's design, 5 in. (12.7 cm) were added to the frame between the seat and the neck. At the same time, the angle of the neck was changed from about 30 to 38 degrees.

Unlike the earlier FXR chassis, which carries its battery in the center of the frame, the Harley-Davidson engineers located the Dyna battery on the outside under the seat. Creating a bike with a sleek profile meant re-location of the battery to an inboard position, which proved to be harder than you might think.

Making room for the battery meant removing structural members under the seat, crafting a new inboard battery box, and then re-engineering the entire area in order to replace the lost strength.

By moving the battery inside, it became possible to fabricate a wraparound sheet metal cover that looks like an oil tank. However, creating a gas tank with a long sensuous shape required more detailed fabrication.

The front fender, from Jesse James, wraps close to the 19 in. Avon tire. The rear tire is another Avon gumball, one size larger than stock, covered by a modified Harley-Davidson fender with a fabricated Cycle Fab taillight. Application of the very red House of Kolor paint was done by Russ and Dave at Cycle Fab, though the graphics are the work of Nancy Brooks.

Left The rake of the frame really puts the 19 in. (48 cm) Perewitz wheel out in front. Note the Headwinds headlight and small panels crafted to fill the void where the gas tank drops over the frame tubes.

Above The bottom three fins were cut off the cylinders prior to the polishing. Though many of the current custom Harleys run forward controls, this Dyna retains the stock mid-glide position.

These Stalker billet aluminum rims are more of David's design work, manufactured and distributed by Sullivan Brothers in Hanson, Massachusetts. The 4-piston brake calipers, carved from billet by Arlen Ness, provide the slow while adding to the show.

East Coast engine man Wayne Lofton decided to increase the horsepower without changing the engine's basic displacement. Thus the Harley-Davidson cases, flywheels, cylinders, and heads were all retained. The Wiseco angle-top pistons, the

Left **Increases in compression, breathing, and ignition ensure that this 80 ci (1, 311 cc) motor performs much better than its stock counterpart. The polished fins contrast nicely with the red paint on the factory heads and cylinders. Even the CompuFire starter is polished to a bright shine.**

Crane camshaft, and the shape of the ports in the Harley heads are all new. A Quick Silver carburetor takes the place of the stock Keihin, while a pair of Bub pipes were chosen to replace the stock, staggered duals.

Externally, the engine is fully polished, with hexed cylinders, Perewitz rocker boxes, and Arlen Ness primary and cam covers. The 5-speed transmission offers more of the same – a polished case filled with back-cut RevTech gears and a Perewitz cover.

At the back, David swapped the stock shock absorbers for a pair of 11 in. (28 cm) Works shocks with aluminum bodies. In front, billet triple trees clamp the factory fork tubes and painted lower legs, equipped with Progressive springs.

More of the stock parts were swapped for the latest offerings from the aftermarket during the final assembly. The handlebars and grips are from Arlen Ness, while the headlight is a beautiful billet piece from Headwinds. The custom seat is of course from Danny Gray.

Full Speed Ahead

Model: Dyna

When David Perewitz' friend Tommy D approached him to build a new bike, David saw it as a chance to try out some of his new prototype products.

Through good timing or good karma, Tommy turned out to be the first person with the new line from Dave Perewitz. The new line includes the prototype 18 in. (45.7 cm) billet wheels used at either end, carved from billet aluminum by the Carriage Works. The front wheel is supported by David's fork assembly consisting of smooth lower legs that work with factory 41 mm fork tubes and internal components. The mid-glide triple trees that clamp those tubes are also part of the evolving line of Perewitz parts.

The front brake is made up of a single, 4-piston GMA caliper which is matched to a floating rotor. The real news in the brake department, however, comes from the the back of the bike. Factory bikes and most custom machines put the rear brake

Right **The trend of late is single-sided front brakes and a rear brake on the left side. David and crew narrowed this Arlen Ness frame in the area under the seat and achieved a different look.**

on the right, while in the case of the new Perewitz prototype brake and pulley assembly, the brake is located on the left. The caliper is anchored to the swingarm, and clamps a rotor that bolts to the inside of the rear wheel pulley.

The frame for the new prototype machine is a Dyna-style frame from his friend Arlen Ness. The frame that Arlen shipped from California to Massachusetts came with 5 in. (12.7 cm) of stretch and a 35 degree fork angle. To spice things up a little,

David had the swingarm chrome plated, then masked off the front half, and had it sand blasted so that part of the swingarm would have enough texture to hold paint.

The gas tanks and center dash are the work of Jed, chief metalman in the Cycle Fab shop. Both front and rear fenders came from Jesse James, owner of West Coast Choppers. With

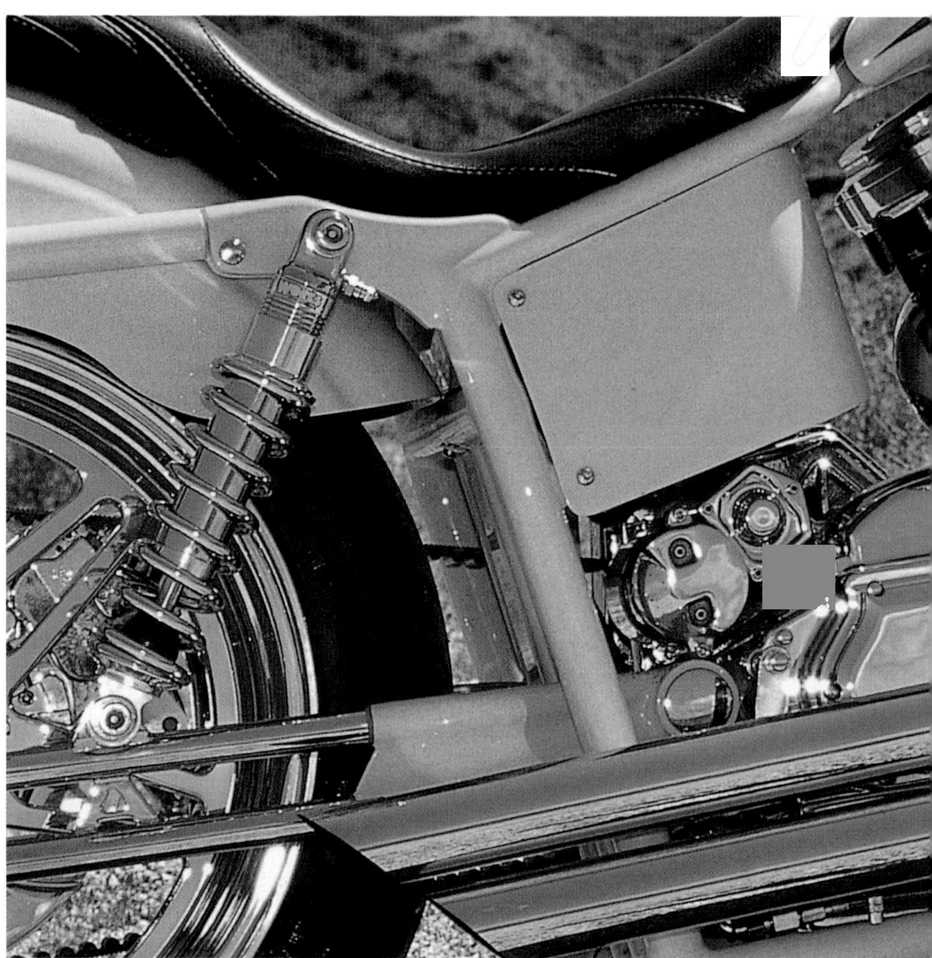

the exception of the chrome-plated half of the swingarm, all the sheet metal and chassis parts are sprayed with a retina-burning yellow urethane paint from House of Kolor. Due to a

Below **The yellow Dyna uses a 96 ci (1,573 cc) S&S mill for power, equipped with a Crane cam and Samson exhaust pipes. Rocker boxes are David's own, as are the transmission side and top covers.**

mishap on one of the bike's first outings, most of the machine has actually been painted not once, but twice. The original molding and paint, as well as the second paint job, are the work of Dave's brother Donnie and Russ Keene at the Cycle Fab shop.

The V-twin that resides below the long stretched gas tanks is a 96 ci (1,573 cc) mill that David bought unassembled from S&S. Before assembly could begin David sent the cases, cylinders, and heads out to be polished, then had the fins on the cylinders and heads masked off so both could be painted a deep blue. Once the paint was dry, Jim Thompson began assembling the parts into a running whole. Jim chose a Crane camshaft for the big S&S engine.

Perewitz rocker boxes cap the S&S heads, while the cam and primary covers are from Arlen Ness.

Above Right **The critter on the tank is a hamster. The owner of this yellow ride is a member of that hallowed group of fun loving, custom bike enthusiasts. Side covers are new, crafted to fit the narrowed frame.**

Right **Engines are becoming an integral part of the bike's visual package. Note the deep blue paint which contrasts nicely with both the polished fins and the yellow paint.**

The new coil bracket on the left side with CompuFire coils is another of David's new products. Samson pipes stretch back past the polished 5-speed transmission, equipped with the new billet top cover. The transmission side cover is really part of David's new hydraulic clutch assembly, powered by a Billet Concepts master cylinder on the handle bars.

The new yellow bike is a fast ride, 0 to 60 in less than 5 sec. That's almost as fast as the Harley-Davidson aftermarket, which has gone from stone-dead to full-speed-ahead.

S&S

Built for Show – and Go

Model: FXR

The Harley-Davidson FXR frame makes a good foundation for a bike that is both fast and easy to ride. The rubber mounting means the engine can vibrate without shaking and wearing out the rider.

With the battery located under the seat, this same frame provides a sleek profile that customizers like Andreas “Fietje” Friedrich can easily improve upon. Though it’s fairly common to stretch a frame and thus enhance the long, lean profile, Andreas stretched his to the limit and beyond. The area between the neck and the seat is now 5 in. (12.7 cm) longer than it was stock. At the same time, the fork angle was increased to 36 degrees, and the swingarm was extended an additional 3 in. (7.6 cm) as Andreas was not content enough with a bike only 5 in. (12.7 cm) longer.

To complement the bike’s long lines, a stock one-piece gas tank was stretched to fit the longer frame. At the back, a fabricated tail-dragging fender covers the spoked wheel and reaches nearly to the ground. Under the seat is another fabricated item that people usually fail to notice.

Right **Tiller style handle bars mount to short risers. Billet grips and chrome switch housing help to clean up the bars.**

Stock FXR's have an oil tank that protrudes into the area just behind the rear cylinder. The oil tank on this FXR is contained within the frame, so the area behind the cylinder and above the starter is much more open and exposed.

Though nearly all FXR's use hydraulic front forks, Andreas chose to use a springer fork to help lower the bike. The Progressive shocks used at the rear are also shorter than stock, so both ends of the radical red ride sit very close to the asphalt.

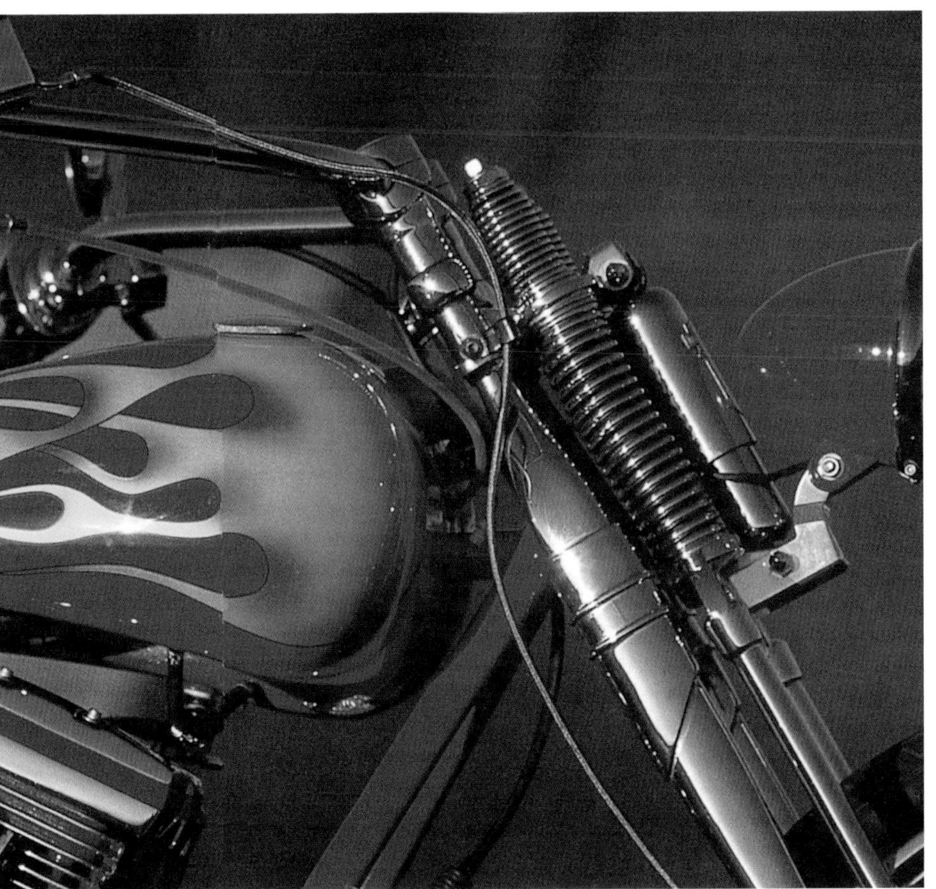

The red rocket's heart is an 80 ci (1,311 cc) V-twin made up of Harley-Davidson flywheels housed in polished factory engine cases. The aluminum Harley cylinders have also been polished and then painted, and house Wiseco 3.5-pistons. Cylinder heads from the king of porting, Jerry Branch, top off each cylinder, the Manley valves are operated by a Head Quarters camshaft. An SU constant velocity carburetor feeds gas and air, and a pair of Bub pipes provides non-restrictive exit to the atmosphere.

Immediately behind the V-twin is the factory 5-speed transmission, connected to the motor by a Primo belt drive. Power leaving the transmission passes through the Barnett clutch to the drive chain, and

Above* Long tank isn't just stretched, it's stretched and shaped to arch over the chrome and painted rocker boxes. *Horst Rösler.

***Right* Crane HI-4 ignition fires a high-output coil hidden behind the factory cover. Note the polished cases, and the neatly polished and painted cylinders and heads. Oil coolers mount to the frame's lower downtubes.**

on to the 170x18 in. rear tire. To slow the bike down, a factory-style caliper in front and an 8-piston aluminum caliper from Hot Shot on the rear wheel were used.

The solo seat is from Gido, the grips are from Arlen Ness, and the billet taillight is from Pro One.

Flying Tiger

Model: FXR

To provide more power for Autobahn use, German engineer Christoph Madaus from Cologne made a series of refinements to the 80 ci (1,311 cc) V-twin, starting with the addition of an SU constant-velocity carburetor and Hypercharger air cleaner.

The precision of single-fire ignition is handled by the Dyna S ignition system. Instead of hiding the high-output coils behind a cover, Christoph left them hanging out in the breeze on the bike's left side, along with the voltage regulator.

For the front, a 43 mm Ceriani fork assembly was mounted in aluminum Ceriani triple trees.

By making his own brackets, Christoph was able to mount two 4-piston Performance Machine brake calipers to the lower legs of the Italian fork assembly. The fabricated brackets locate the calipers where they can best clamp the large-diameter floating rotors. The front wheel combines an Akront aluminum rim with a wheel and hub from WiWo. Wrapping the rim is a Bridgestone 100x18 in. tire.

This international motorcycle with the Italian forks and Japanese tires uses French shock absorbers from Fournales. Unlike conventional shocks wound with a spring, the Fournales units use a cushion of high-pressure air to support the back of the bike. The

Left **High-performance coils mount in the area normally shielded by a side cover. Voltage regulator mounts just behind the coils.** ***Horst Rösler.***

Right **Serious brakes: twin 4-piston calipers are coupled with large diameter floating rotors. 18 in. tire mounts to an Akront rim, bolted to a disk-style wheel.**

lower end of these slick shock absorbers bolts to a massive aluminum swingarm with eccentric axle adjusters made by WiWo. The swingarm supports a somewhat unusual rear wheel made up of a WiWo hub and disk coupled to a Akront rim. Mounted to the rim is a 140x17 in. Bridgestone tire. Instead of the factory belt, Chris chose chain drive to the rear wheel.

The fabricated front fender is another of Christoph's creations, as is the small air dam bolted to the frame behind the front wheel. The rear fender is a modified factory fender; the gas tank is also a made-in-Milwaukee item.

The handlebars mount to the top triple trees with short risers, both the bars and the risers have been modified so all the wiring runs inside. Turn signals have been located at either end of the handlebars, just outboard from the billet grips.

The turquoise paint job is by Nicolay in Cologne, while the airbrush work is by Becker Design in Nieder-Olm. The Flying Tiger logo on the tank brings back images of brave men in leather jackets flying high-performance aircraft.

Left* High-performance brakes and suspension make this a more functional Harley-Davidson FXR. Note the unusual oil tank and trim front fender. *Horst Rösler.

A Family Affair

Model: FXR

It might be genetic that both Richard Seals and his daughter Debbie make their living in the airline industry.

And it might be Nature who dictated both would ride motorcycles. But it's strictly luck that both ride customized Harley-Davidson FXR's. After meeting Grady Pfeiffer, diehard custom enthusiast and sales representative for various aftermarket companies, Debbie decided to get her stock FXR a makeover.

When father Richard Seals heard that someone was "improving" his daughter's FXR, he too decided that his own stock FXRT with saddle bags and tour pack, needed a whole lot of improvement.

For Debbie, the next step-up came when the engine on her FXR gave trouble. Bartels Harley-Davidson pulled the engine out to repair the bottom end, and while the engine was out, Grady and his friend Howard Stubbins took the bike home to their shop.

Once they had the frame bare, Grady and Howard took it over to Kevin Seawright, who increased the fork rake to 38 degrees and molded all the welds. Next the frame, swingarm, and the lower legs were painted black. In place of the factory wheels, a new pair of billet aluminum hoops were installed, a 16 in. (40.6 cm) at the back and a 19 in. (48 cm) in front. The front rotor shares the design seen in the rims, coupled to a chrome-plated factory-style caliper.

Bolted to the frame is the trick rear fender with the unique light assembly, done by Famart Welding. The front fender is simply a molded factory fender. Likewise for the gas tank, which resembles a stock tank minus the dash, with a flush-mount cap. Over the whole thing is a very bright paint job by Phil Stadden in Torrance, California. Danny Gray supplied the seat while the Arlen Ness catalog supplied the bars and many of the accessories.

Richard's bike was similar to that of Debbie's in several departments,

Right **Debbie and her father Richard consider themselves lucky: both love motorcycles, both ride great-looking FXRs, and both love to spend the first week of August with thousands of friends in Sturgis, South Dakota.**

except for the chrome-plated GMA brakes, the polished and painted factory wheels, and of course the candy red paint used on both the sheet metal and the frame.

While both bikes use "leaned on" 80 ci (1,311 cc) motors for power, Richard's uses a Crane camshaft with 0.600 in. (1.5 cm) of lift, mated to 10.3:1 compression Dave Mackie ported heads. Debbie's Bartels-assembled V-Twin, on the other hand, relies on the more common and less radical Sifton 141 cam with 0.480 in. (1.22 cm) of lift, working in harmony with the 9:1 compression heads ported by Fast Eddie. For carburetors, Bartels chose to stay with the stock CV carb,

while Howard picked a butterfly style Series E mixer from S&S. Both use Bub pipes.

Externally, both engines use painted and polished cylinders combined with high-quality chrome-plated cam and primary covers. Differences include the fully polished cases used on Richard's bike and the different air cleaners.

Above **A hotter hot rod 80, with 10.3 to 1 compression, a high-lift cam, and S&S Super E carburetor.**

Prowling Australia

Model: V-Twin

The current enthusiasm for V-twins and the shortage of bikes in many Harley dealerships throughout the world has led to a thriving clone business.

Anyone and everyone is setting up shops to become a motorcycle manufacturer. In small quantities the process isn't too tough: take your pick of an aftermarket frame and engine, add accessories, assemble carefully, and put your own imprint on the gas tank. In the case of the Prowling Australian, however, the approach was different. The attempt was to build a better V-twin motorcycle, one that takes advantage of the V-twin power and torque, without the traditional limitations in ground clearance, handling, and weight. The result is the Prowler, a uniquely Australian V-Twin motorcycle that combines the power and torque of a V-twin engine, with the light weight and handling normally associated with bikes from Europe or Japan.

Though the Prowler might look at first like just another Softail, a closer

Left **Taillight housing mounts to the rear inner fender, while the turn signals bolt to the aluminum seat-strut. Wherever possible Trevor specified lightweight parts manufactured in Australia.**

Above **V-twins and twisty roads don't have to be mutually exclusive. With adequate ground clearance and suspension travel, the Prowler is a big bike that actually handles the curves with ease.**

look reveals that instead of using two shocks under the transmission, this bike relies on a single White Power shock hidden under the seat. The unusual frame is fabricated in Australia from chrome-moly tubing according to specifications and drawings provided by Trevor and Gary Flood. Up front, the well-supported neck area supports an upside down White Power fork assembly. The net result is a strong lightweight frame with more ground clearance and suspension travel.

The Prowler is designed for both speed and comfort. Rather than bolt the engine and transmission directly to the frame, the frame uses a Dyna-style rubber mounting system for the engine and transmission. But the use of a Dyna drivetrain has another advantage. Dyna 5-speed transmissions mount the oil tank for the engine under the transmission, not under the seat. Production Prowlers will use a transmission case cast from magnesium as a means of further reducing total weight.

The twin goals of light weight and high quality are both met by producing the bodywork in-house. The gas tank, ducktail, fenders, and side covers are all produced from either Kevlar or carbon fiber. A neat aluminum housing mounts the speedometer and tachometer in the center of the tank. In order to keep as much of the production as possible in Australia, many of the parts that can't be produced in-house are sourced from local firms.

The 88 ci (1, 442 cc) engine is the one item that couldn't be found in Australia. The S&S components are, however, assembled into a running whole. For exhaust a stainless-steel two-into-one system from Staintune, another Australian company, was chosen. A primary belt is used to carry the power to the transmission, where close-ratio Andrews gears deliver the torque to the output pulley. Another belt carries the power to the unusual 17 in. (43cm) rear wheel. Like the frame, the wheels are designed by the Flood brothers and produced locally. The spun aluminum design was chosen as a good combination of strength and light weight. Both wheels measure 17 in. (43 cm) in diameter, the front is 3.5 in. (8.9 cm)

wide while the rear is a full 4.5 in. (11.4 cm) in width.

A pair of 6-piston Performance Machine calipers and huge 13.5 in. (34.2 cm) floating rotors give the Prowler brakes as good as those found

on any Ninja or Ducati. Because the front brakes do nearly all the braking on a hard stop, the rear brakes use a single 4-piston PM caliper and a smaller rotor. Thus Australia's first Super Bike, the T38 (Australian Prowler), was born.

Above **Sourced mostly in Australia, the Prowler combines modern looks and high-quality components with a traditional V-twin engine. Note the unique sheet metal of the aerodynamic front fender and sleek rear inner fender.**

Edelbrock
PERFORMER R.P.M.

Dressers

Known as Dressers or Baggers, there seem to be more full-dress Harley-Davidsons on the streets each year – and a large percentage of them are modified or customized. Perhaps it's the baby boomers going slower with more comfort. Perhaps these bikes are finally getting the recognition they deserve. The people at Harley-Davidson aren't the only ones participating. All the major catalog companies have a wealth of new parts designed specifically to improve the looks of the big Harley.

The parts run the gamut from lowering kits, to trim pieces that fit between the bags and the fender. Dressers are becoming seamless and sophisticated.

The Dresser phenomenon seems to be subtractive-customizing: people tend to modify and simplify the bike by taking things off. That way the nice lines and the good basic design of these kings of the highway can shine through.

There was a time when nobody but your uncle would be caught dead on a Dresser. But those days are gone. Now it doesn't matter because Dressers are so cool, everybody wants one.

Here are five bikes: a much modified road king, three different interpretations of "standard Dresser customizing," and a Dresser as seen through the eyes of Arlen Ness.

The Latest Thing

Model: Road King

Like most of his bikes, Joe Procopio bought his Road King at Cycle Craft Harley-Davidson in Everette, Massachusetts.

With help from the crew at Cycle Fab, Joe stripped the new bike down to nothing but a bare frame sitting on a packing crate, surrounded by the stock fenders, wheels, drivetrain, and all the other parts that make up a complete motorcycle. In place of the Milwaukee iron, Joe ordered a front and rear fender from Jesse James, then asked his friend Jed from Cycle Fab to fabricate a taillight housing and install it in the bottom of the rear fender.

The tank was cut up until there was little of the original left, and then it was brought back until the tails on either side almost touch the side covers.

Donnie and David, the brothers Perewitz, were convinced to paint the bike in a tangelo color from House of Kolor. Not only did the boys paint the sheet metal, they went for a bit of the Euro-look by painting the headlight nacelle, fork assembly, dash, and even the fender struts in the same tangelo hue. Nancy Brooks then did the graphics before Donnie laid on the final clearcoats.

The only changes made to the motor are the Bub pipes, which still contain the full complement of packing and baffles.

The turn signals and switches on the handle bars were retained. At the front, small oval clearance lights bolt to the headlight nacelle, and function as unobtrusive turn signals. At the back, aftermarket clearance lights function as blinkers. Painted to match the bike, they almost disappear into the rear fender struts. While the taillight is set into the fender, the license plate bracket bolts to the swingarm on the left side.

For wheels, new 16 in. (40.6 cm) aluminum assemblies from Dave Perewitz, with a 130 series tire on the front and a 140 on the rear were chosen. The rear shocks are the stock length, though they bolt to a swingarm

Above Right **A Jesse James rear fender houses a Cycle Fab taillight. By painting the clearance lights and bolting them to the fender struts, the rear turn signals become an integral part of the bike instead of just an add-on.**

been inverted to drop the back of the bike about two in. (5 cm). The use of the flipped swingarm and an aftermarket fork assembly up front means the whole machine sits lower than stock, but not so low that the frame is dragged on speed bumps and driveways.

Having shed off all that extra bulk, including brackets, windshields, and saddle bags, the new bike looks almost like a slightly oversize FXR.

A Canadian Eye Opener

Model: Dresser

The extensive sheet metal work on this bike owned by Michael Ethier of Maschouche, Quebec, includes the front fender that nearly drags the asphalt, the tanks that reach back to blend with the frame, and the thin strips of chrome plate that decorate the side covers and bags.

Daniel Lauzon from Montreal is the man responsible for the extended front fender and the tails on the tanks. While extended tanks have become fairly common, less common are the chrome rails that rise up between the top of the bags and the fender, and the shock absorber covers that you see between the fender and bag when you look at the bike from the back.

The neat little chrome strips are the work of the Bozzini Machine Shop in Montreal. Each strip was manufactured from steel before being shipped off to the chrome shop. They aren't glued on, but are held in place by small screws that come in from the back side.

The highly detailed V-Twin features four different colors of powder coat, contrasting with the polished fins and abundant billet. Deshaies Cycle in Montreal disassembled the engine so the various parts could be polished and/or powder coated. Arthur Tiberyan, the mechanic at Deshaies Cycle who did most of the work, installed an S&S carburetor and a pair of Bartels pipes, but left the engine otherwise stock.

Most of the engine accessories are from the Arlen Ness billet aluminum line. The air cleaner, lifter blocks, pushrod covers, rocker boxes, cam cover, derby, and inspection covers, are all from Arlen's catalog.

Though there's plenty of billet aluminum on Michael's bike, he chose to retain the stock cast 16 in. (40.6 cm) wheels at both the front and the back. The factory wheels have been polished at the edge of the rim, and then powder coated to match the paint on either end of the bike. Metzeler tires in stock 130/90x16 in. sizes mount to both rims.

Right **The factory wheels are different colors to match the different paint on the opposite ends of the bike. Airbrush work is extremely nice, note the stainless trim on the edge of the windshield.**

A pair of Jay Brake 4-piston calipers mounts to the front fork legs, while the stock caliper is retained at the rear. To lower the bike in the front, the fork tubes were cut 2 in. At the rear, a White Brothers kit is used to bring the back of the bike down a similar amount.

Bob Morin from St. Hubert, Quebec, applied the white and purple paint and Sylvain Beliveau from Montreal did the very intricate graphics with an airbrush. With acres of sheet metal and fiberglass, Dressers provide the ideal canvas for a talented painter.

The bars, switches, grips and mirrors all carry the Arlen Ness logo. Though the taillight is from Arlen's catalog, the small lights including the

Above **The engine in Michael's Dresser displaces 80 ci (1,311 cc) and is essentially stock on the inside. Outside, however, it's a different story. Done in four separate colors, the engine is all polished aluminum and powder coat.**

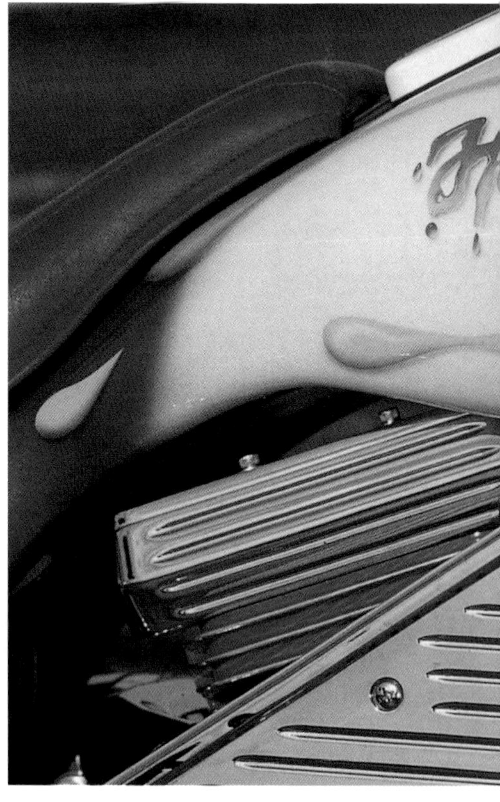

Right **The billet rocker boxes, pushrod covers, tappet blocks, and all the rest carry the Arlen Ness logo.**

blinker lights that have been set into the bags use lenses from the Custom Chrome catalog.

But perhaps the cleverest trick on the whole bike, one most people don't even notice, is the windshield. If you look carefully, you see that the chrome strip that circles the policestyle windshield isn't a chrome strip at all. The chrome strip, and even the screw heads, are actually more airbrush work from the talented Sylvain Beliveau. With help from fellow Canadians, Michael Ethier has built a unique Dresser. Whether it's the bright paint, the quality accessories, or the fabricated parts, it all works to make one bright Harley-Davidson – a bike that is rightly called a real eye opener.

A "Dresser" from Arlen Ness

Model: Dresser

Amidst all the success that now surrounds Arlen Ness, it's easily forgotten that he is in essence a custom motorcycle builder.

The bikes Arlen Ness calls his Luxury Liners started as Convertibles – bikes he conceived to be two bikes in one. By removing the fairing and swapping the full fenders for the smaller fenders that came with the bike when it was ordered, a person could convert the bike from cruiser mode to bar hopper in an afternoon. The trouble with the two-for-one concept lies in the success of the full-cruise mode. The bikes are so comfortable, with the fairing to keep off the bugs and the bags to provide a place to put a few necessities, that no one ever took off the full-dress outfit.

So what we have is an Arlen Ness Luxury Liner: a Convertible turned Dresser. Arlen thought that if people were using them as Dressers, why not go all the way and provide a tour pack so people can really tour on these long-legged highway bikes.

Right **Arlen sells these Luxury Liners in limited quantities, or you can build your own from catalog parts. A frame stretched 5 in. (12.7 cm) makes for a long comfortable bike.**

Underneath the fairing, bags, and tour pack is an Arlen Ness Dyna-style frame with five inches of stretch and a 35 degree fork angle. Dyna-style is translated as rubber-mounted in the fashion of the Dyna models. The frame itself is made from 1.25 in. (3cm) mild steel tubing, though the signature twin-rail swingarm is built from chrome-moly tubing.

Though the Arlen Ness catalog is filled with the latest billet aluminum

wheel designs, most of the Liners seem to come with spoked wheels. Specifically, a pair of 18 in. aluminum rims laced to Arlen Ness hubs. The hot setup is to install a 170x18 in. tire at the back, which actually makes for a slightly wider end result than a 180, when used with a 5.75 in. rim.

The billet is bolted to the front frame, and the mid-glide triple trees from the Ness catalog clamp a pair of shortened 39 mm fork tubes. At the back, two 12.5 in. aluminum-bodied shocks hold up the signature twin-rail swingarm.

There is no Arlen Ness motor (at least not yet). 80 ci (1,311 cc) Luxury Liners use mostly Harley-Davidson internal components mounted in polished S&S cases. The bike shown here uses the larger displacement option, a 96 ci (1,573 cc) polished S&S engine with Edelbrock heads, a Carl's camshaft, S&S carburetor, and a two-into-one SuperTrapp/Ness exhaust.

The 96 from S&S uses the full line of in-house polished billet parts. On the right side, the cam cover, tappet blocks, pushrod covers, and two-piece rocker boxes are all from the catalog. On the left, the chrome-plated outer primary carries the Arlen Ness logo. The transmission is adorned with the same kind of billet jewelry, including the top cover, and the right side cover which also houses the slave cylinder for the hydraulic clutch mechanism.

Right Carl Brouhard is responsible for the graphics package. Turn signals are integrated into the stalks of the mirrors.

These bikes get their distinctive looks from the sleek fairing and lowers, an original Arlen Ness design. It's interesting to note that the headlight still mounts to the fork and not the fairing. This made it possible to pull the fairing off without removing the headlight during conversion to convertible mode.

Taildragger fenders do a good job of protecting the rider in any kind of inclement weather and provide the bike with nice lines. The unique bags and tour pack provide the storage needed by one or two riders out for a day or a week. Between the neck and the Danny Gray seat is the long, one piece gas tank, hand formed from sheet aluminum.

Unlike some of the stripped-down customs, these bikes come with the full complement of switches on the bars. Look closely and you find they even have turn signals, the front lights incorporated into the mirror stalk and the rears built into the fender strut.

The purple and white paint job is the work of Arlen and Jon Nelson, with wild graphics by Carl Brouhard.

Edelbrock
PERFORMER R.P.M.

No More Bad Luck Charm

Model: 1990 FLH

Some of the changes made to this FLH are more obvious than others, but the total effect is to clean up the bike without a radical change in character. Most obvious among all the missing parts is the tour pack and the stock windshield. Less obvious is the missing stock turn signals for both the front and back of the big Dresser. In front, the blinkers are mounted flush at the outer edge of the factory fairing, while at the rear the turn signals are set into the lower corner of the saddle bags.

A Fat Boy front fender was mounted down nice and close to the 16 in. Dunlop tire, using the mounting bracket from the stock Dresser fender. Sparkling chrome-plated spoked wheels replaced the cast Dresser wheels. The V-Twin was stripped down to bare cases, and then everything was sent out for polish and paint. Ed's Polishing in Landover, Maryland, put a bright shine on the factory cases, took the bottom three fins off the cylinders before polishing the remaining fins, and also shined up the fins on the Harley heads.

The engine upgrade included a fresh valve job for the heads, high-compression Wiseco pistons for the cylinders, and stock Harley components inside the engine cases. An Andrews camshaft and adjustable pushrods take the place of stock components, while a Super E

Left **The deep color is kandy brandywine from House of Kolor. Graphics might fall into the currently popular "tribal" category. Tribal or not, they are very, very bright.**

Above **Most of the covers on this side are simple chrome covers from Harley-Davidson. Even though these use rubber-mounted engines, many riders still use cushioned floor boards to further reduce the effects of vibration.**

carburetor from S&S with matching air cleaner takes the place of the Keihin CV carburetor. Most of the engine covers are simple chrome-plated components from Harley-Davidson, though billet lifter blocks and pushrod tubes are from Arlen Ness. On the right side a two-into-one Thunderheader takes the place of the usual stock Harley-Davidson exhaust system.

The stock 5-speed transmission went through a simple inspection and rebuild, with back-cut gears for easier shifting. Unlike the engine cases, the transmission case is painted to match the rest of the machine.

Final sheet metal improvements include an extended rear fender and a mildly stretched stock gas tank with matching dash. All the sheet metal modifications are the handiwork of Bart Poole.

Preston Doyle from Doyle's Customs applied kandy brandywine from the House of Kolor and then did the unusual and very colorful graphics. Even the seat, made especially for the bike by John Longo of Rockville, Maryland, is stitched in colors that match the kandy paint job. After masking off the fins, Preston used the same shade of kolorful kandy to paint both the cylinders and heads.

Before the project was complete, a few more parts were swapped. The fork uses tubes one inch shorter than stock, and the front brakes use chrome-plated factory calipers. To match the drop in front height, White Brothers shock absorber brackets are used to lower the back of the bike.

Left Harley-Davidson Dressers tend to look better and better as owners take more and more of the visual distractions off the bike. By removing some of the lights and accessories, the basic design of the bike is able to shine through.

A Police Cruiser Turned Custom Harley

Model: Police bike

The bikes we call Dressers come in various forms, everything from Road King to Ultra Hog.

The bike seen here started life as a police bike, complete with fairing, extra lights, and saddle bags with big round release knobs on top.The sophistication of the design starts at the very front of the bike where an Arlen Ness fender wraps around the 18 in. Metzeler tire and extends almost all the way to the asphalt. Just above the fender the headlight is mounted in a Road King headlight nacelle. The gas tank, based on the original, seems to start pretty far forward on the frame, and then extends all the way back to the side covers. The two-tone color scheme that begins at the headlight nacelle runs across the gas tank, and continues across the saddle bags. The bags are capped with fiberglass covers with a shape intended to mimic that of the rear fender.

Right **Terry's clever sheet metal design and paint make for a very appealing bike that doesn't use much of the standard billet jewelry.**

Below **Doug and his partner at speed in Nevada.**

To convert this one-time pursuit vehicle, Steve Stonez stretched the frame 4 in. (10 cm) and increased the rake to 40 degrees. Little things make a big difference here; in this case, the frame was raked and extended in such a way that the neck actually moved closer to the front gas tank mount.

Bob at Carefree Highway Truckin' in Tulsa extended the tank. He then proceeded to wrap the tank around the front of the seat, and extended

Left **The Taildragger fenders add to the extreme experience of riding a bike that seems to almost merge with the asphalt. Like most Baggers, this one looks good with dual exhaust.**

the tails down to almost merge with the side covers.

The small seat is the work of Eric Long, who also did much of the assembly of the sleek former police bike. Between the saddle bags is another Arlen Ness taildragger fender, equipped with a specially-designed trick LED taillight. The Pro One billet wheels measure 18 in. (45.7 cm) on both ends. The front tire is a 140/70x18, while the back is a 150/70x18. Both front and rear brakes use single factory-style calipers coupled with stainless-steel rotors designed to match the wheels.

In spite of the fact that the engine was in pretty good shape, a little warm-up seemed to be in order. For a boost in compression, A.M. Levvinskie from Tulsa installed a pair of Wiseco 10.5 to 1 pistons, a Crane camshaft, and an S&S Super E carburetor. The air cleaner cover from Sumax adds style, as do the Bartels mufflers, and the Pro One billet engine covers.

The final assembly included a White Brothers lowering kit in the front fork and shorter shocks at the back.

From black and white, the cruiser went black and sandstone. A former pursuit vehicle is now being pursued at every event by photographers and onlookers.

Index

HARLEY-
DAVIDSON